CELEBRATING READER MINISTRY

Dr John Murray *(on right)* at Selwyn

CELEBRATING
READER MINISTRY

125 years of lay ministry
in the Church of England

RHODA HISCOX

MOWBRAY

Mowbray
A Cassell imprint
Villiers House, 41/47 Strand, London WC2N 5JE, England

First published 1991

British Library Cataloguing in Publication Data
Hiscox, Rhoda
  Celebrating reader ministry:
  125 years of lay ministry in the Church of England
  1. Church of England. Readers
  262.15

ISBN 0–264–67211–9

Phototypeset by Input Typesetting Ltd, London
Printed in Great Britain by Biddles Ltd, Guildford and King's Lynn

Contents

Foreword

'Like a mighty army moves the Church of God . . .' or should it be 'Like a mighty tortoise'?

Rhoda Hiscox has given us a splendid account of 125 years of Reader ministry, and we are greatly in her debt for all her research, reflection and presentation. What saddens me, from this account, is to see how desperately slowly changes have taken place, and there are some strong lessons here for the whole Church. The deep opposition to lay ministry, described in this book, still lingers on! Here we read of the lay Reader (in Chester diocese!) who received the offering but had to leave the plate on the floor outside the sanctuary, being forbidden to enter; here we see the arguments, the battles, the reluctance and long processes to acknowledge, authorize and encourage the ministry of Readers. The wearisome and drawn-out opposition to women Readers has a lot to teach us in the argument about women priests today. So much of what we now take for granted and think reasonable – like Readers assisting in the distribution of Holy Communion and preaching their own sermons – did not happen easily.

It is significant that the revival of Reader ministry was on Ascension Day (in 1866), the day when we recall the Ephesians statements of the variety of ministries given by the ascended Lord to the Church. How impoverished the Church would have been had lay ministry not been developed, trained and used in it. Rhoda Hiscox rightly challenges the wording of the ordination service, which she finds painful because of the non-recognition of lay ministry, in its statements that all lay people are sheep to be led. It is amazing that there is no service for the Admission of Readers in the ASB even though the plea for such a service in the Prayer Book was made in the 1930s. It must happen in the next revision – and hopefully will be of higher quality than many Diocesan Admission Services.

The importance of women's ministry in the Church – wider than Readers – is handled by Rhoda Hiscox with considerable care; there is also the hope expressed that there will one day be a woman on the staff of every parish. The demand for Readers to be allowed to baptize must be agreed soon by the Church. There are many developments happening, and Rhoda Hiscox is right up to the minute in her grasp of where we are and where we hope to be in Reader ministry.

Readers are a wonderful force in the Church – and will be increasingly effective with the training requirements now being instituted. They should be great preachers – with a relevant touch of 'knowing the thoughts' of the lay people. As Rhoda Hiscox rightly says, all and not some diocesan Readers' Boards must now stop looking inward and become far more outward looking in ministry, mission, evangelism and care. The 125 Celebration in 1991 is, for all Readers, a moment for looking back, giving thanks and celebrating, but it is also a moment for going forward in a fresh way in this vital ministry for the Church – indeed, going forward as 'a mighty army'.

Rt Rev. Michael A. Baughen
Bishop of Chester
August 1990 Chairman of Central Readers' Conference

Preface

The ministry of Readers is the only lay ministry in the Church of England which is voluntary, nationally accredited, episcopally licensed, and governed by Canon. This book aims to celebrate 125 years of the ministry of Readers, and to show how that ministry has developed from uncertain beginnings in 1866. There are now more than 8,000 Readers, a quarter of whom are women. Recently the number of Readers admitted each year has been greater than the number of people ordained. Readers can no longer be considered a 'stop-gap' ministry; in some dioceses it would be impossible to maintain Sunday services in every church without them. While of particular interest to Readers, past, present and future, this book has a wider purpose, and is intended for all who are interested in the ministry and mission of the Church of England.

I have used inclusive language throughout, except where it would have been inappropriate. As women Readers were not admitted until 1969, much of the book is concerned with male Readers in a Church almost entirely organized by men.

Many Readers have contributed to this story, some of them unknowingly, and some who wrote to me following a notice in *The Reader*. I am most grateful to them and to many others who have helped me in various ways. The Chair of Central Readers' Conference, the Rt Rev. Michael Baughen, and its Executive Committee, encouraged me to go ahead at a very early stage, though this is not an official history but a personal perspective on the past, present and future development of Readers. The staff of the Church of England Records Centre, Dr Brenda Hough, the Rev. Ian Pearson and Mr Edward Pinsent made my task much easier with their cheerful and unfailing help and interest. Dr Anthony Dyson, Professor of Social and Pastoral Theology in the University of Manchester, has been a kindly mentor, and Canon Timothy Tyndall, recently Chief Secretary of ACCM, has also encouraged me. My thanks are also due to my friend and former colleague, Miss Wendy Harris, who gave generously of her time to decipher and type my manuscript. Finally, as a

Reader myself, I owe much to my Reader friends in the Diocese of Rochester, and to my own vicar, the Rev. Alan Vousden, and my three Reader colleagues at St Mark's, Bromley, for much encouragement and kindly forbearance during the past few months.

Rhoda Hiscox
May 1990

Abbreviations

ACCM	Advisory Council for the Church's Ministry
CRB	Central Readers' Board
CRC	Central Readers' Conference
DRB	Diocesan Readers' Board
LOM	Local Ordained Minister
MSE	Minister in Secular Employment
NSM	Non-Stipendiary Minister
PCC	Parochial Church Council

I have used the more popular title 'Warden' throughout as less cumbersome than 'Warden or Bishop's Adviser'.

I have also referred to 'Readers' and 'Reader ministry' with a capital R to distinguish them from all other readers. No disrespect is intended to other ministers!

Acknowledgements

The author and publishers are grateful for permission to reproduce the following:

Second Collect for Pentecost (p. xiii) from *The Alternative Service Book 1980*, and extracts from *All Are Called* (pp. 106, 110), by permission of the Central Board of Finance of the Church of England. Extract from letter (p. 101) by permission of Teresa Parker.

Almighty God,
who on the day of Pentecost
sent your Holy Spirit to the disciples
with the wind from heaven and in tongues of flame,
filling them with joy
  and boldness to preach the Gospel:
send us out in the power of the same Spirit
to witness to your truth
and to draw all peoples to the fire of your love;
through Jesus Christ our Lord.

(Second Collect for Pentecost, Alternative Service Book)

1: Not only on Sunday

Every Sunday in parish churches throughout England over 8,000 men and women, in cassock, surplice and blue scarf, may be found taking part in leading worship. These are Readers of the Church of England. Alongside clergy they may share in the ministry of the Word at Holy Communion, including reading the Gospel and preaching. Alongside other members of the laity they may share in reading the lessons, leading prayer and intercessions, and assisting with Communion. In many churches Readers are responsible for leading Morning and Evening Prayer, apart from the absolution and blessing. Indeed it is only through the ministry of Readers that some churches are able to have a service of worship every Sunday.

Who are these Readers? They are men and women of all ages, drawn from all walks of life, who have experienced the grace of God in their lives, and whose gifts have been recognized by clergy and congregation in their local parish. All have had their call to serve God through a public, lay ministry tested by a process of selection, followed by a period of training in their spare time, usually for two or three years. They have been admitted to the office of Reader and licensed to work in a parish by the bishop, usually at an annual gathering of Readers in the diocese. At the Admission Service they are given a New Testament, and in many places their incumbent places the blue scarf on the new Reader. Depending on their personal gifts and individual circumstances, and on the needs of the parish, Readers primarily exercise a preaching and teaching ministry, together with pastoral work and other forms of lay leadership. All have to work out their call to serve God as trained and accredited laypeople as they grow in their faith within a changing Church and a changing society.

The Reader story is one of God's grace, of vision and commitment, of gifts and skills shared in unstinting service, of dedicated work in extending God's Kingdom, of outgoing love and sometimes painful vulnerability. Conversely, it is a story with many shadows; of a minority of Readers with little learning combined with much arrogance, of the defensiveness of those seeking to guard well-marked boundaries or clinging to office because they cannot accept that God has other servants able to fill their place.

What has been true of the Reader movement has been true of the institutional Church. On the one hand it is a story of bishops and clergy whose vision of the priesthood of all believers has led them to encourage Readers to share their essentially *lay* ministry with priests and deacons to further the Kingdom of God. On the other hand, it is the story of the reluctance of other bishops, clergy and laypeople to allow Readers to respond to liturgical and pastoral needs which therefore had either to remain unmet, or to be served by disregarding existing regulations, though usually with the good will of the clergy concerned. For the whole people of God, Readers and clergy and laypeople, disappointment has alternated with hope, tension with trust, frustration with fulfilment.

The name 'Reader'

The name 'Reader', which is derived from the 'Lector' of the early Church, hardly describes the range of Reader ministry today. 'Lay Preacher', 'Lay Minister', 'Lay Curate' and other titles have all been considered and rejected for various reasons, and no one has yet suggested a name which is universally acceptable. Among Readers themselves there seems to be a general feeling in favour of living with the title, despite the ambiguity. Among congregations 'Lay Reader' persists. In context 'lay' seems to locate the Reader in the Church as distinct from the ordained minister, while at the same time pointing the Reader to the world outside the Church.

In 1984, the Bishop of Newcastle, then Chairman of the Advisory Council for the Church's Ministry, called upon Readers to live up to their name and become 'the Church's lay theologians, thinking, well-informed, articulate . . . lay men and women . . . theological resource persons'. While a few Readers are theologically better qualified than their clergy, others feel that 'lay theologian' suggests a sophistication they would not wish to claim. Nevertheless, as people called to exercise a preaching ministry in a changing world, Readers cannot escape the necessity for reading and informing themselves, for thinking, for expressing thoughts coherently and in terms others may understand, and for bringing the resources of faith to bear upon life, and relating life to faith. Bishop Graham was pointing to resources that Readers bring to a world where Christianity appears to be dying through ignorance rather than informed rejection. By presenting Readers with this challenge to live up to their name,

Bishop Graham gave Readers new confidence to exercise their particular ministry alongside other ministers, lay and ordained.

The Canons provide the framework within which Readers may operate. Canon E4 *Of Readers* states that

> A lay person, whether man or woman, who is baptised and confirmed and who satisfies the bishop that he [*sic*] is a regular communicant of the Church of England may be admitted by the bishop of the diocese to the office of reader in the Church and licensed by him to perform any duty or duties which may lawfully be performed by a reader . . .

The Canon outlines Readers' duties, which include visiting the sick, and generally undertaking pastoral and educational work to assist the minister. Liturgically, Readers are permitted to read Morning and Evening Prayer (save for the absolution), to publish banns of marriage, to read the Word of God including the Gospel at Holy Communion, to preach including preaching at Holy Communion, to receive and present the offerings of the people, and to distribute the holy sacrament of the Lord's Supper. Readers may also bury the dead.

Canons E5 and E6 relate to the nomination, admission and licensing of Readers. Under Canons B43 and B44, Readers are given authority to minister in churches of other denominations to the extent that they are licensed to minister in their own.

Two comments on the Canons are necessary. First, although they set out the duties for which Readers are authorized, the bishop of the diocese draws up the licence of what a Reader may do. In some dioceses therefore Readers are not yet permitted to distribute the bread at Communion, nor are they allowed to conduct funerals. Secondly, the Canons themselves reflect the Church's need of, and growing confidence in, the ministry of Readers. For example, to begin with Readers were not allowed to preach in consecrated buildings, and at first they could only read sermons written by others. Almost every duty now permitted was derived from pastoral need, often for more than a generation before the Canons embodied the thinking and practice of the Church.

A kaleidoscope of Reader ministry

As a typical example of the varied patterns of Reader ministry I have chosen the Diocese of Salisbury, where, at the end of 1989, there were 116 men and 27 women Readers with a further 50 men and six women who, having reached the age of 70, were no longer licensed but have the bishop's permission to officiate. According to their annual returns for 1989, about a third of the active Readers preach less than once a month, but some of these administer the chalice almost every week. The other two-thirds preach at least once a month and are very active. Some preach and lead Evensong, Mattins or non-liturgical services weekly or fortnightly, assist regularly at Communion, lead intercessions and read the lessons. About a tenth of the Readers have taken funerals during the year, some on several occasions. Many lead study or prayer groups and take the sacrament to the housebound. These activities represent the heart of Reader ministry.

The category of 'other work which you consider to be part of your overall ministry' resulted in a fascinating glimpse of Readers at work. For example a few Readers exercise a prayer ministry and lead meditations. Many are involved in worship during the week as well as on Sunday. They minister at homes for the elderly, they train and rehearse groups in music and drama for worship, participate through the laying-on of hands at healing services, prepare family services, and undertake the work of sacristan or verger. Work with children and young people, including holiday clubs, and acting as cathedral chaplains, bring Readers into contact with people outside the Church.

Pastoral work, especially visiting, is very high on the list of priorities. Hospital visiting can be very time-consuming when the hospital is 30 miles away. Counselling is undertaken by those with appropriate training. The range of pastoral work also includes visiting the dying and bereaved, making 'distress' calls at the incumbent's behest, working alongside disturbed and distressed young people, having oversight of the pastoral needs of the village and 'visiting, listening, telephone contact and correspondence'.

Training covers a wide variety of tasks including baptismal preparation, pre- and post-confirmation preparation, training servers, organizing training days for various groups including a Business Men's Fellowship, chairing the deanery Lay Pastoral Assistants' Training Committee and speaking at women's meetings.

The involvement of Readers in the maintenance of the ecclesiastical institution is impressive. One is a member of General Synod, and several serve on diocesan and deanery synods, and their committees, often as officers. Readers act as Chairs, Secretaries, Treasurers, Conveners and members of committees as diverse as the Bishop's Council, the Diocesan Liturgical Advisory Committee, the Board for Social Responsibility, the Diocesan Mothers' Union, the Readers' Committee and an Archdeaconry Ecumenical Committee. In the parishes there are a plethora of Parochial Church Council sub-committees often chaired by Readers. During an interregnum one Reader took total responsibility for the teaching and pastoral care in the parish, including ministry and outreach to a semi-Urban Priority Area.

Happily, not all the energies of Readers are church-centred. They help to organize clubs for the elderly, bingo in one parish, and a holiday scheme for American visitors in another. One is a prison visitor, another is secretary of 'Cancer Contact' working with the terminally ill; a third directs a local neighbourhood help scheme; two visit newcomers to their villages and welcome them. Some are governors of local schools and colleges, including a theological college.

Some Readers have particular gifts, and as musicians, writers and artists, contribute to the life of the wider community. One helped to plan 'A Celebration of Food and Farming'. Many Readers use their professional training in work, which may be full or part time, or on a paid or voluntary basis. Several are teachers, two or three teaching religious education to A level and encouraging Christian groups in school. One of the primary head teachers offers pastoral support to children, their families and the staff when need arises. One reader is an honorary solicitor to a professional organization; one helps to run a home for homeless men; one is a member of HM Prison Service; one is Diocesan Director of Education, another the Area Secretary for Christian Aid.

The range of work undertaken by Readers in Salisbury diocese is typical of the contribution of Readers to the life of both Church and community. Salisbury is by no means exceptional; it has a smaller number of Readers than many dioceses. Lichfield has over 400 Readers; only five dioceses, including Sodor and Man, have fewer than a hundred Readers. Multiply the work of Salisbury Readers by the 44 dioceses and you have some idea of the place of Readers in the life of the Church of England. Reader ministry takes place not only on Sundays, but on every other day of the week. Can the Church survive without its Readers?

The ministry of individual Readers enriches the life of the Church in countless ways. A few are licensed as assistants to hospital or prison chaplains, or serve in these and similar institutions during interregnums or as a regular part of their parish duties. Some serve in HM Forces, both at home and abroad. A small number of Readers are licensed for stipendiary lay work. Six are employed by the Missions to Seamen; others in industrial missions and in ministry to the deaf. One Reader, profoundly deaf herself, has gathered a small band of sensitive helpers and exercises an imaginative ministry from a church base which has become a community centre for the deaf and deaf-blind. In this friendly meeting place one may discover a deaf choir, a women's devotional meeting, or a group of young adults whose colour and deafness lay them open to much misunderstanding in the community, and who find help and understanding at the centre. Another Reader is employed in very different circumstances, in an Urban Priority Area in the north. He works full time for the church to which he is licensed but is given a small allowance by the local authority. He thus identifies with the poverty of those among whom he works in a pioneering ministry.

More than 99 per cent of Readers are voluntary. A few glimpses of their ministry cannot do justice to the diversity of Readers' ministry. Nevertheless they are included as pointers to the gifts and experience of life they have among them, but which is domesticated, even suffocated, by much of our church life. Contrast the research marine scientist standing on the deck of a ship on a clear starlit night with no other ship in sight, filled with awe at the majesty of the Creator, with the young opposition councillor in an Urban Priority Area asking how, if we take the Incarnation seriously, we can shut ourselves away from issues of homelessness, racial harmony and economic regeneration. A doctor sees his patient 'not just as a machine which is not functioning properly, either from some part of the organization malfunctioning or from some disharmony (disease), but as a living whole, created in the image of God'. A hospital gardener tends his plants with equal care, walking miles along the corridors of a busy hospital, firm in the knowledge that he too is contributing towards wholeness and healing. One 87-year-old is still active in the suburbs, having given almost a thousand showings of slide-sets on a variety of topics, every one of which has a Gospel message woven in.

In a rural area in the north a small village with a scattered population of 250 had an average congregation of eight in a church attached to the parish church of the adjacent country town. A retired Reader who moved into the area became the virtual pastor of the village, responsible for the liturgy apart from Communion. In less than ten years the congregation trebled, a house study-group now meets, a broadsheet is delivered with the milk, and when funds were needed for a new heating system they were oversubscribed. There is an increasing awareness of the needs of others, and a growth in self-respect. Relations with the parish church are good, and the Reader attends staff meetings. In this parish, as in other rural areas, people much prefer the ministry of one Reader whom they come to know well to a series of peripatetic Readers who remain virtual strangers.

Many Readers find it very difficult to draw a line between what they do as Readers and what they would do anyway as lay Christians.

Some feel that they spend 'far too much time in churchy circles and churchy things'. Others engage in a delicate balancing act. For example, one person discovered that being a Reader took on new meaning when her secular employment as a school nurse was transferred to the parish where she lived. Parents are pleasantly surprised to meet her at medical inspections in school, but avoiding expectations of a 'surgery' at the church door is sometimes problematic. In her combined role she is invited to take school assemblies from time to time. She is convinced that her Readership has not only enhanced her interaction with the world, but has enabled God to be an acknowledged presence.

Where the shoe pinches

Many Readers encounter theological and ethical challenges in the course of their ministry and work. The examples which follow indicate how a few Readers have tried to relate their faith and their life, and suggest that here is a resource which the Church might call upon more frequently in its interaction with society. Sometimes actions speak louder than words. During the 1984 miners' strike an area coal board official went to court to speak in support of striking miners who he felt were being unjustly treated.

One Reader wrote an article for his professional paper taking a personal view on two important ethical issues in his industry. The first concerned responsibility to the community. He argued for encouraging goodness, truth and beauty as part of our national heritage in design, instead of promoting social engineering and expressions of personal manifestos. The second drew attention to ways in which professional expertise and commitment were being devalued by shoddy workmanship and the use of inferior materials, to the detriment of both professionals and the public. The article concluded with positive suggestions for overcoming morally indefensible practices. Three results followed. The article led to some immediate interesting enquiries relating to the Reader's beliefs; he found himself exercising a telephone ministry 'as word comes to me from various sources within our industry of people in need of support'; and when speaking to various professional groups he is often called upon to field questions relating to his particular faith and position.

An industrial chaplain spends about a quarter of his time in pastoral work with employees and their families, not only supporting them, but trying to pinpoint conditions at work which may have led to their present suffering. His main work lies in the day-to-day visiting of workplaces, to affirm what can be affirmed and to question what cannot, in terms of 'justice, peace and the integrity of creation'.

> The agenda is that of the poor and disadvantaged, not in any hostile way, but in an attempt to ascertain *who* is responsible for questionable policies, the reasoning behind them, and whether they are likely to have the slightest idea – or interest – in the side-effects of these policies.

Underlying this is a Christian model of compassion, service and setting people free. The great theological themes of creation, incarnation and redemption provide the criteria against which all human action must ultimately be judged, whether its effects are intimate, corporate or global.

> Our secular society has uncoupled the everyday world from the life of faith . . . The task of the industrial chaplain (along with many other people) is to show that this divorce is unrealistic, and, indeed, damaging.

These Readers are typical of those who find that the shoe pinches as they tread paths at work which are critical for their understanding and interpretation of their faith, and their witness to it. They may arrive at different answers for similar problems and cope in different ways, but they know that because of their Readership they are marked people. Conscious of their own shortcomings, it is at these points that they often become conscious too of the infinite grace of God.

The shoe pinches in a much more practical way for some Readers, especially the under-45s, who find themselves under pressure at times from the competing claims of home, job and Reader ministry. Clergy and congregations often make too many demands on Readers. It is not always realized that Readers may elect to undertake different duties at different times; they do not have to do everything at once. While the role of a Reader is said to be as long and as wide as he or she cares to make it, there are times when a 'sabbatical' may relieve the pressure and bring much needed refreshment and renewal.

Relations with the clergy

As a lay ministry, good working relationships with the clergy are obviously desirable for Readers. While clashes of personalities do occur from time to time, in the majority of parishes there is give and take on both sides. There are still clergy who are so used to having sole control in the parish that they are very nervous of

Readers, but their numbers are gradually dwindling, and younger incumbents are generally more willing and able to share parochial responsibilities. Where there is mutual recognition of gifts and opportunities to work from strength and to develop new skills, both Readers and clergy grow in their respective ministries. Readers are part of the staff of the parish and are increasingly joining staff meetings, and in some places deanery chapters, on a regular basis.

It is not always realized that on a change of incumbent a Reader's licence must be endorsed on the recommendation of the incoming minister, usually after a settling-in period. If a prospective incumbent has no wish to work with a Reader then both he and the bishop should recognize that that parish is not for him. There is no excuse for Readers discovering within a month of a new incumbent's arrival that 'my new vicar does not want me'. While accepting the sensitive nature of clergy–Reader relationships, clergy have for too long been protected from situations which Readers have learned to take for granted in industry and commerce, where staff have to be lived with in creative tension. Readers too need at times to be more open to change, and to accept new ways of doing things so that relationships may be allowed to grow, perhaps in unexpected ways. Shared ministry works both ways.

Wardens and Bishops' Advisers

There is one group of ministers (until recently always ordained clergy), to whom Readers are especially indebted, namely the Wardens or Bishops' Advisers for Readers. On behalf of the bishop they have the oversight of Reader ministry in their respective dioceses, usually in addition to a parish, diocesan or cathedral appointment. Where there are two or three hundred Readers in a diocese, this may add considerably to their workload. Diocesan organization varies; some Wardens are assisted by Sub-Wardens who may be responsible for the Readers of an archdeaconry. As well as acting as links between bishops and their Readers, they are also links between the diocese and Central Readers' Conference through their annual meetings hosted by the Advisory Council for the Church's Ministry. This gives an opportunity for thinking to be shaped between the dioceses and the centre, and for the mutual exchange of information. In many regions it is customary for Wardens to meet together to share their concerns, and increasingly, their resources.

Wardens are responsible to the bishop for the selection, initial training, and licensing of all new Readers. They usually chair the Diocesan Readers' Board which oversees the practical arrangements for enabling and supporting Readers in their training and service. As well as being involved in the pastoral care of Readers, particularly those under pressure, they may have to sort out problems when these arise between Readers and their incumbents. A little 'sanctified common sense' often goes a long way on these occasions, unless the difficulties are more serious. In-service training of Readers may be arranged by Wardens or their deputies, often in collaboration with the diocesan Continuing Ministerial Education Officer. As well as representing the bishop to the Readers, the Warden may also need to represent the Readers to the bishop, as a way of integrating Reader ministry into the life of the diocese and encouraging the provision of better resources.

Most Wardens give their Readers far more than the Readers have any right to expect. There are, however, some areas where, with a little more imagination (and perhaps a little more time were it available), Wardens might take some initiatives which would bring great benefit to the Church and to Readers. For example, Wardens are very well placed to spot Readers with unusual gifts and skills and to encourage them to use these more widely. Many Readers can relate how they have attended training sessions and have squirmed at the amateur fare provided, knowing that they or their colleagues have professional expertise in the same area, which they would willingly share. Such expertise might also be made available in wider Church circles.

But not only in church! A Warden who knows the area well might also encourage Readers to extend their ministry beyond the church walls into the local community. Such suggestions may assume a greater awareness than the Warden might have opportunity to acquire, and a greater readiness on the part of Readers to look beyond the immediate scene or to give yet more time which can ill be spared. Even so, it is when confronted with the unexpected challenge that we are brought face to face with the claims of the Kingdom of God.

Among the Wardens who were kind enough to share their thoughts I should like to quote two, one from a rural and one from an urban diocese.

Readers need and deserve plenty of support and encouragement. Whether they receive it or not is a rather hit-or-miss business. We have some difficulty with in-service training, and this is in part due to a reluctance by the Church to provide the resources. Readers give their ministry voluntarily . . . I think we ought to put more into continuing education, which would give them a sense of support, as well as providing fellowship and stimulation, and which would give us an even better ministry.

My dream is that the increasing interest in lay ministry will release the clergy to be enablers of the ministries of the whole Church in ways many of them never dared to believe would happen. God's frozen people released to be God's people on fire for him, and Readers as the bellows fanning the flames . . . !

Not only on Sundays

This chapter reflects Reader ministry as it is being exercised throughout the Church of England. It has described only a small portion of the whole picture. Both the lighter and darker sides of Reader ministry interplay from time to time in the pages which follow. As Readers mark the 125th anniversary of the revival of their office in 1991 they – and the Church of England – have much to celebrate as they offer their praise to God.

2: Beginnings

The office of Reader was first revived in 1561 by Archbishop Parker. Readers in the reign of Elizabeth I ministered in poorer parishes 'destitute of incumbents'. They were permitted to read the appointed service 'playnlie, distinctlie and audiblie' but not to preach or interpret. They were allowed to bury the dead and purify women after childbirth, but not to administer the sacraments or 'other public rites of the Church'. In their personal lives they were to be sober in apparel, especially in church, to read a chapter of the Old Testament and New Testament daily, and to 'move men to quiet and concord, and not give them cause for offence'. Readers were never very numerous, but there is some evidence that the office was exercised here and there in the North of England until the mid-eighteenth century (G. Lawton, *Reader-Preacher*, Churchman Publishing, 1989, chapter 9).

The revival of the office of Reader
The revival of the office of Reader, at a formal meeting of the Archbishops and Bishops of the provinces of Canterbury and York at Lambeth Palace on Ascension Day 1866, was the culmination of a series of debates which began with the revival of the Convocation of Canterbury itself in 1852. The Convocations of Canterbury and York were the two provincial assemblies of the clergy of the Church of England, which had not met for the conduct of business since 1717.

As early as 1853 the Ven. W. H. Hale had advocated utilizing the services of devout and competent laymen not merely on Boards of Finance, but in the services of the sanctuary. This demanded that 'some must qualify themselves for this high and holy work', while all must believe in the prophethood of the laity and consequently accept the services of any of the people of God, whether lay or clerical, seeing that both were endowed with the Spirit and duly commissioned by the Church.

A report on the Extension of the Diaconate in 1859 was followed by one on 'Lay Agency' five years later. Both reports and debates reflected the inability of the Church to cope with the rapidly increasing population, which rose from nine million in 1801 to twenty million in 1861, especially in the new industrial areas. The clergy, too, were unevenly distributed, with many in the south and too few in the north.

The Bishop of Lincoln estimated the need for 300 extra clergy every year, even though he admitted that the Church lacked the money to pay them. He queried 'whether there is not a large amount of zeal which can be turned and directed to greater good among the laity'. A solution which would disturb the ecclesiastical system as little as possible, increase the working power of the Church at little expense, and license men under the authority of the bishops and the direct control of their incumbents, was attractive to clergy and laity alike. Whether these assistants to the clergy were to be lay agents, sub-deacons, lay deacons or lay teachers or Readers continued to be debated, but the bishops decided to use the name 'Reader' when they sanctioned the office.

Underlying the debates was a growing concern, especially among evangelicals, for the moral and spiritual well-being of the poor. 'Every day convinces me more and more that some such organization is necessary to reach the great mass of our people' said the Bishop of London.

In a thoughtful paper entitled 'On the Proposed Office of Readers' (read at a meeting of the Ruri-decanal Chapter, Bradford-on-Avon, May 1867), the Rev. Edward Meade justified the revival of Readers by drawing attention to the needs of scattered rural hamlets as well as the towns where the population 'by *force of numbers* overpowers the abilities of the Incumbent'. He maintained that in many parishes ministerial power and ministry work appeared to be evenly matched, while the true position was that the work had been laid out and undertaken so as to suit the existing power, and not so as to supply the actual need, leaving much work undone, even unattempted. Meade, who approved of Readers, raised the question of which course is the safer:

> Is it safe to leave the work in our parishes undone, or very inadequately done? Is it safe to leave multitudes of those who have been committed to our charge, to be fed with spiritual food by *anybody* or by *nobody*? Is it safe, considering the best interests of the people and congregation over whom we are appointed, to serve them in the House of God with a languid, meagre and defective ministry, when, by accepting and improving such an

agency as that of Church Readers, all this might be greatly remedied?

Readers, working in partnership with clergy and laity, have been attempting to 'remedy' the situation ever since. As confidence in their ministry has grown, so the range of their work has been gradually extended, by resolutions of the Convocations of Canterbury in 1884 and York in 1889, by regulations in 1905, 1921, 1941 and 1969, and by amendments to Canon law.

Who were the early Readers?

Though the Resolution agreed by both Houses of the Convocation of Canterbury in 1884 stated that the title should be simply 'Reader', 'Lay Reader' is commonly used, perhaps to distinguish Readers from those who are called upon to read the lessons in Church. Readers were confirmed and communicant members of the Church of England, nominated by the incumbent (and in some dioceses also by two laypeople of the parish), and willing to sign a Declaration of acceptance of the doctrine of the Church of England as contained in the Book of Common Prayer, and of obedience to the incumbent and 'other properly constituted authorities', subject always to the control of the bishop.

Many of the earliest Readers were already doing the work for which they were being licensed. As teachers and catechists they were working in Sunday schools and with young people, often conducting cottage and schoolroom lectures or Bible classes, and holding short services on Sundays or week days in rooms not usually employed for public worship. The Bishop of Bangor, speaking in Convocation in 1884, wanted

> Christian men who can bridge over the gap between the different classes of society; who, being in close communication with the clergyman on the one hand and the industrious masses on the other, can interpret each to each.

They were to be men with strong, earnest minds, who knew their Bibles, possessed a ready power of vigorous speech, and who could be a source of new strength to the Church.

The first Reader in the Church of England is thought to have been J. D. T. Niblett, licensed to the parish of Standish in the diocese of Gloucester. He was one of a number of well-educated medical men, barristers and gentlemen of independent means, who formed a core of Readers commissioned to speak or preach in their dioceses. Some of them were instrumental in breaking down the social barriers which existed in the Church, either directly, like Earl Nelson who only agreed to become a Reader if 'every grade or society' might also become Readers, or indirectly, like the town clerk of Louth who preached regularly to a large group of navvies every Sunday afternoon.

While the Dean of Manchester claimed in 1894 to know from experience that the poor were extremely particular as to the calibre and class of men who ministered to them, most Readers were 'more in unison with the masses with whom they mixed'. Described as the better educated from among the uneducated, they were godly men who knew, in the words of the Bishop of Bangor, 'the thoughts that are passing in the hearts of our mechanics and artisans and labourers, their struggles and their difficulties . . . and the causes which had hitherto kept them back from going to Church' (Convocation of Canterbury, 13 February 1884). Many were teachers trained in Church colleges. Others were skilled craftsmen or tradespeople whose faith and zeal were such that, had not the Church of England utilized their service, they would have found a hearty welcome among the Nonconformists.

By the beginning of the twentieth century different classes of Readers had already emerged. Most common were *Parochial Readers* with a licence from the bishop, valid for a single parish on the nomination of the incumbent. *Diocesan Readers* were usually well educated and commissioned by the bishop to officiate in any parish at the request of the incumbent. Gradually *Scriptural Readers* and *Catechists* or *Teachers* were given Reader licences. Many of these were based in mission halls with a very limited sphere of work, often Bible classes and Sunday schools. Unlike other Readers they worked full time, usually for a pittance and without any kind of security or prospects. More numerous were groups of *Lay Evangelists* or *Lay Preachers* which had begun to proliferate and function independently until Convocation resolved to include them under the Reader umbrella in 1897.

In 1889 the Society for Promoting Christian Knowledge opened a Layworkers' College in Stepney, to provide a year's training for 36 men at a very modest cost. Before the College closed in 1924 over 600 men, of whom a third became Readers, had been trained. They were usually admitted as Readers by the Bishop of London, and then licensed by the bishop of the diocese where they were to work.

In 1892 Wilson Carlile founded the Church Army, thus gathering together many local groups in the Church of England who had adopted the methods and spirit of the recently established Salvation Army. By 1905 there were 1,034 trained workers, all licensed as

Readers. These lay evangelists trained for a year in London, studying the Bible and Prayer Book and practising their preaching in Hyde Park and the London slums. Soon they had about fifty horse-drawn caravans touring cities and countryside conducting missions. Church Army officers, who were the only group of Lay Evangelists to survive, continued to hold Reader's licences until 1976 when they came directly under ACCM's Accredited Lay Ministry Committee.

A third group, known as the Lichfield Evangelist Brotherhood, had its centre in Wolverhampton, where men trained for three months followed by a probationary year. Of 34 who had trained by 1896, fourteen remained in the Lichfield diocese and the other twenty were serving in dioceses overseas. Gardeners, footmen, painters and compositors were among those who gave up their jobs to serve God and to spread the gospel among working people. As stipendiary Readers, Lay Evangelists were licensed either as diocesan or parochial Readers.

What did these Readers have in common? Undoubtedly the early Readers were earnest and zealous servants of Christ, committed to spreading the faith among their contemporaries from a Church of England base. More formally they were described as men of moral character, faithful in their religious life, sound in doctrine and with a gift for imparting religious instruction. Some went to immense trouble. A Northamptonshire man, two miles from the nearest church, fitted up a room above his stables so that he could be licensed to serve there as a Reader. A Lincoln Reader regularly took an afternoon train to Woodhall Junction station, whence one of the congregation ferried him across the River Witham and accommodated him after the Sunday evening service as there was no return train, and he returned to Lincoln by carrier's cart early on Monday morning.

From the early 1880s many Readers were drawn into diocesan fellowships where these existed, but for most it was a lonely life. While some clergy suspected, possibly with some justice on occasion, that the glib tongue of the Reader tended to undo their patient work, others realized that if the layman was good at his work he generated among the people a need for the clergy. Wesley had succinctly expressed it more than a century before: 'Use talent and you have talent'.

Lay curates, lay preachers

The Official Year Book of the Church of England for 1903 records 2,375 licensed Readers, 1,663 in the Province of Canterbury and 712 in York Province. While some of these undoubtedly held 'ornamental' licences and did no more than read the lessons in Church (for which no licence at all was required), the great majority devoted much time and energy in the service of the local parish.

In 1904 a report on *Readers and Sub-Deacons* (Convocation of Canterbury, no. 383) formed the basis of new Regulations drawn up by the Archbishops and Bishops in 1905. These regulations did not have the force of law, but they set out the principles on which all forms of Reader ministry – diocesan, parochial, evangelist and catechist – might function. The title 'Reader' was affirmed, thus building up the reputation of Reader ministry as a lay office.

The regulations introduced a common form of *Admission* to the ministry of Reader with the delivery of a New Testament, but without the laying-on of hands, and a separate *licence* authorizing the Reader to work in parish or diocese. This marked another step forward. It gave the Reader national recognition and avoided the system whereby some Readers who had moved from diocese to diocese were admitted several times and collected several New Testaments! Laymen were permitted to read duly authorized parts of the Litany and Morning and Evening Prayer (omitting the absolution and blessing) in consecrated buildings. Licences to preach were to be be given with great caution, and only on assent to the Thirty-Nine Articles, in order to fulfil the provisions of the 1662 Act of Uniformity. But Readers were not allowed to preach when an ordained minister of the parish was present. No lay officer was to preach during the Communion service or from the pulpit. The 1905 regulations promoted the further development of Reader ministry, though progress remained slow and piecemeal.

But people like Bishop Yeatman-Biggs, successively Bishop of Southwark and Worcester, encouraged Reader ministry whenever they could. Writing in *Lay Work and the Office of Reader* (Longmans, Green, 1904; Handbooks for the Clergy series), he described Readers as 'lay curates' and 'lay preachers', and envisaged 'a field of happy, holy usefulness and activity' open to the Reader. He was often able to go where the clergy could not go, and do what the clergy could not do. He could take the burden of a hundred details off clergy shoulders. Teacher, almoner, server, choirmaster, the Reader might be found in Sunday schools, in clubs caring for young men and boys, in the choir, the belfry, the cricket field, and sick rooms.

Similarly *The Reader and Lay Worker*, a monthly magazine first published in January 1904, reflected the needs of Readers. The first volume contained several articles on Sunday schools, including a series of Children's Addresses with titles as varied as 'Lay Hold on Eternal Life' and 'A Michaelmas Daisy'. General principles for start-

17

ing The Young Men's Club were suggested. There was very practical advice on Football and Cycling Clubs, and how to start and equip a Gymnasium with ten pounds. One article described experimental work among men for their spiritual and moral advancement. 'Men, working men, think deeply, and can be helped . . . in a way which would not so much help women and children' (vol. i.6, p. 110). Two articles expressed differing views on Temperance. In the first issue a Rochester Reader gave basic advice on Lantern Services which still holds good for users of modern technology today: 'Be sure of your lantern and screen', and, even more important, 'Raise the exhibition of lantern pictures to the level of Divine Service instead of bringing Divine Service down to the level of the Sunday School Treat' (vol. i.1, p.18).

No doubt with such varied demands on Readers in mind, Bishop Yeatman-Biggs concluded his book with a note of caution. While all were members of the Spirit-bearing Body of Christ, the standard must not be set so high that likely men were deterred from starting. Work must be linked with prayer, and enthusiasm with restraint, so that Readers did not undertake more than they could properly do.

Critics of Readers were quick to resort to legal arguments. The ministrations of Readers were neither 'legal nor desirable'; they had no legal status within the Church of England. Some argued that they were debarred by the twenty-third Article of Religion, that only a man 'lawfully called and sent by men who have public authority given unto them in the Congregation' might preach in Church. Others maintained that the Pluralities Act of 1838 which forbade clergy to engage in a profession or trade or deal in goods or merchandise, also prevented Readers from ministering in church. During the second half of the nineteenth century the Church of England tended to be legalistic in outlook, owing to the ritualistic and ceremonial conflicts with members of the Oxford Movement. It was not surprising, therefore, that the lay office of Reader, as it began to develop, should also be the subject of legal scrutiny.

Much discussion centred on the question of Readers, however well qualified, conducting services and speaking in consecrated buildings. In the Convocation of Canterbury in 1884 it was suggested that Readers should be allowed to preach after normal services, when the church would otherwise be shut up and the poor shut out. But the poor were unlikely to attend Morning or Evening Prayer in church, especially where the existence of pew rents banished them to the remoter parts of the building. The Book of Common Prayer, too, was a barrier for those with little or no formal education.

In the Convocation of York Bishop Goodwin of Carlisle thought that the further they could go in the direction of using laymen within the churches the better it would be for the practical efficiency of the Church, and he wondered how best to use the laity's zeal and willingness to help. A bishop of an urban diocese where there was much new church building was so exasperated that Readers would be debarred from ministering in them that he reflected whether or not he would consecrate the buildings when they were ready!

In 1894 the Archbishop of York wanted to make better use of parish churches when they would otherwise be closed and dark. He envisaged additional services of a simpler kind with 'no intention to interfere with ordinary services for faithful Church people'. It was not until 1921 that it was suggested that 'the real consecration of the churches would be by the character of the ministrations offered in them, and the devotional use of them by the congregation.'

Diocesan Readers, who were usually well educated, were gradually permitted to preach in church. At first it was customary for sermons to be given 'after services'. As the Book of Common Prayer made no provision for sermons at Morning or Evening Prayer, when a Reader was preaching there was a pause to signify the end of the service. After a brief interval the Reader's sermon followed. London diocese led the way and some Readers began to preach from time to time following Evensong. During World War I the Bishop of Manchester stated that he had no objection to Readers preaching at evening services, and that by doing so they would establish a precedent for the post-war years. At the Annual Conference on Readers' Work in 1918 a carefully worded resolution was passed suggesting that, as a consequence of the war, authority might well be given to Readers so commissioned (the diocesan Readers) to preach the sermon which usually followed Morning or Evening Prayer, if invited to do so.

In the early days of Reader ministry much preaching took place in the open air. When preaching did begin to take place in consecrated buildings, Readers stood at the lectern. The pulpit was reserved for the clergy as the church's place of authoritative teaching and exhortation. Readers were not formally permitted to use the pulpit until the Regulations of 1941.

What were Readers to preach? At first they could only read printed sermons, or possibly preach someone else's sermon in their own words. From 1904 the Sermon Notes based on the lectionary set out in *The Reader and Lay Worker* magazine for every Sunday in the month proved most popular. It was suggested by one bishop that the Reader might make a good sermon once a month and preach it in several places, on the grounds that George Whitfield had considered that he was never able to preach a sermon satisfactorily for himself until he had preached it five times. Extempore sermons or 'a few words' were denigrated as little thought wrapped up in much words. Some drew a distinction between the layman's ability to instruct the people in Church doctrine, and such topics as the Christian use of capital or Christian socialism 'which were occupying the minds of men' and would, it might be hoped, encourage them to come to church. Few people grasped the distinctive contribution which the lay person might make to preaching and interpreting the Gospel, and the great advantage of laymen preaching on the relevance of religion to business life and kindred subjects.

Readers who were authorized to preach were examined in certain books of the Bible and in doctrine as contained in the Bible and the Book of Common Prayer. One bishop stipulated 'actual reading and preaching before well-qualified critics', while another regarded the mission hall as good practical training experience. London, Rochester, Winchester, Peterborough and Truro (perhaps because of the strength of Methodist Local Preachers) did more to encourage the preaching of Readers than most other dioceses. To those who in 1904 questioned the legality of Readers preaching, the Bishop of Manchester responded that if it were not legal, then the necessary legislation should be promoted.

There were many anxieties still to be allayed. Did the laity want to be preached to by the laity? Some clergy resented lay preachers and claimed they would drive people out of church. One incumbent, who had encouraged 'men of the lower order, earnest, devout and godly men' to preach, found that they failed because the laity did not want to hear. He was, however, honest enough to admit that a certain laywoman in the district was so effective that she drew people' away from church! While some clergy hoped that preaching by Readers would encourage other lay people to come to church, others feared that some might begin to preach strange doctrines, and perhaps end by establishing some sect of their own. For those with eyes to see, however, episcopal commissioning of laymen prepared to preach the gospel to unevangelized masses, would, 'if their labours could be directed and controlled, be full of promise and blessing to the land' (York Convocation, 1885).

Achievements by 1921

After 55 years and a traumatic war, what had been achieved? The 1921 Regulations, which extended those of 1905, provide a good marker of the national position. Before admission would-be Readers had to be recommended to the bishop by the incumbent and lay representatives of the parish. They were examined in their knowledge of the Holy Scriptures, and in the doctrine and practice of the Church as set forth in the Book of Common Prayer, and tested by the bishop or a responsible person on his behalf as to 'their several functions of reading, speaking, teaching, catechising and preaching'.

The Admission of a Reader in one diocese was recognized throughout the world and was not to be repeated should a Reader transfer to another diocese, where he would be relicensed. At the Admission service he was admitted by the bishop 'to the office of a Reader in the name of the Father and of the Son and of the Holy Spirit' and given a copy of the New Testament. There was no laying-on of hands. The bishop was required to keep a list of all licensed (parochial) and commissioned (diocesan) Readers. The licence was revocable by the bishop at any time, or upon the written request of the incumbent. On the death or removal of the incumbent the Reader might continue to hold his licence, should the bishop think fit, during the vacancy, but his new incumbent needed to apply to have the licence renewed or endorsed.

Parochial Readers were permitted to take services and preach in consecrated buildings, but only in cases of necessity and with the special permission of the bishop. Both diocesan and parochial Readers were explicitly *not* authorized

> to take part in the administration of Holy Communion; to administer Public Baptism; to read the Burial Service; to publish Banns; to read the Absolution or to give benediction; to enter the Sanctuary for the purpose of presenting the alms or giving the Blessing; or to officiate at the Thanksgiving of Women after child-birth.

The 1921 Regulations included three growth points, two of which encouraged what was already happening. Readers' Boards or Committees, with representation from the Readers themselves, were to be set up in every diocese (they already existed in about half the dioceses, some from the early 1880s). A Central Readers' Board was to be established to co-ordinate the organization in the diocese, and to maintain and develop the work of Readers generally. Again this built on the achievement of the Annual Conference on Readers' Work and greatly extended its sphere of influence. Thirdly, it proposed 'a voluntary examination for a diploma for Lay Readers', which eventually became the Archbishops' Diploma, the first examination for which took place in 1933.

The 1921 Regulations incorporated much that was already happening and provided a framework for future growth. How it felt to be a Reader in the parish may be judged from two letters published in

The Lay Reader (vol. xviii, 1921). The first, published in January, is from a Southwell Reader.

> Lay Readers in theory are a necessity, in practice they are not wanted by the Bishop, clergy or congregation . . . In most parishes the wealthy layman has priority over any licensed Reader . . . There is a wealth of spiritual fervour, of willing devotion and sacrifice, unrecognized because unwanted . . . Lay Readers have done the greatest service during war difficulties . . . they are waiting to do more, much more if permitted, to help in the greater need of these troublous days.

The second letter, published in June from a Leicester vicar who had been ill for six months, records his appreciation of Readers. 'From the congregation I have heard nothing but praise, and their appreciation of the excellent and practical sermons has been very great and real.' Many priests in the diocese owed much 'to the unselfish and most efficient work of this body of Lay Readers'.

The clergy as a whole showed mixed feelings. Some gave their Readers every encouragement, others were suspicious (occasionally with good cause!) or felt threatened by the gifts of an able Reader. Bishop Lightfoot had spoken in 1884 of the great need of the English Church to employ laymen as laymen, and to enable them to realize that they were members of a royal priesthood. In all dioceses some Readers might be found who, whatever their title or duties, were in the eyes of their contemporaries both sign and anticipation of the royal priesthood of all believers.

3: Towards Recognition and Acceptance

Readers or deacons?

Since the revival of the office of Reader in 1866 there have been recurrent debates about the diaconate, sub-diaconate, 'lay agency' and, more recently, lay ministry. Speaking generally, members of the Oxford Movement put the emphasis on Church order and looked for tidy ecclesiastical systems, while evangelicals stressed lay responsibility and the use of God's gifts in God's service. These were not necessarily in competition, but once the office of Reader had been officially recognized there were differences of opinion as to where, when and how to fit it into the ecclesiastical system, especially within a Church which was trying to cope with rapid change.

In 1884 a report of a Joint Committee of the Convocations of Canterbury and York, *The Diaconate and Lay Readers* (no. 161), proposed admitting to the existing Order of Deacons suitable men of competent education, social status and mature age, who would retain their secular means of support, give their services free of charge, and remain deacons instead of proceeding to the priesthood. York Convocation at first favoured extending the diaconate, but eventually both Convocations agreed a number of resolutions which encouraged the ministry of Readers and placed it on a firmer footing.

Discussion was stimulated by the publication of William Bright's *Waymarks in Church History* (Longmans Green, 1894, chapter x). Bright, who was Regius Professor of Ecclesiastical History in the University of Oxford, allowed that the revival of a permanent diaconate offered the double attraction of an appeal to the primitive standards of the Church, while meeting at no cost the demand made on the Church by an ever increasing population. It was incomprehensible to Bright that anyone becoming a deacon could conceive of consecrating only his 'leisure' to God's service. 'The urgent stress of modern professional life will reduce that "leisure" to very narrow dimensions indeed. An order which is both lay and clerical is neither one nor the other.'

In 1904 both Convocations received another report, entitled *Read-*

ers and Sub-Deacons (no. 383). Both agreed that it was not desirable to restore the Order either of Readers or of sub-deacons as a minor *Order* in the Church of England. Thus by implication Readers were categorized as *lay* ministers and in no way part of a clerical Order.

The trauma of World War I and its grave consequences for manpower again turned the mind of the Convocation of Canterbury to the diaconate. It appointed a Committee whose report (no. 538) in 1921 was entitled simply *The Diaconate*. The main trigger for this further consideration of the subject was the increasing number, during the war and immediately afterwards, both of celebrations of Holy Communion and of people attending them. At festivals where an incumbent had to administer single-handed to a congregation of 800, some people left the church after an hour without ever receiving Communion. The committee made three recommendations: that the diaconate should be restored as an order of the ministry not necessarily leading to priesthood; that the Pluralities Act 1838 should be amended to enable deacons to earn their living by secular work; and that well-considered experiments should be made when and where opportunity offered.

Meanwhile Readers were continuing their varied ministries. *The Guardian*, a church newspaper claiming to be 'thoroughly in touch with cultivated lay opinion', considered the 1921 Regulations as a great advance on those of 1905, but still not going far enough. It advocated discarding such ridiculous restrictions as that upon the use of the pulpit. There could not be too many diocesan Readers, 'men of the professional classes, including men of outstanding eminence in various walks of life, often keenly interested in questions of liturgiology, Church history and cognate subjects'. There were practically no limits to their possible usefulness. Parochial Readers, on the other hand, were drawn from a different social stratum, yet they formed 'an immense reservoir of vocation and power . . . As street preachers, Sunday School superintendents, parish workers in the workshop and the cottage among their own people they can bear witness of the very highest value.' Under the direction of a judicious and sympathetic incumbent they could be most useful (19 August 1921).

The *Church Times* was a little more restrained. The 1921 Regulations were approved as systematizing Readers' status and training.

> The Reader of today is essentially a layman. He looks upon the clergy from the layman's side of the fence, and not seldom with the layman's justly critical mind. Layman he is, and neither clergy nor people accept him as being anything more.

As for preaching, although most attractive to the Reader it was less valuable.

> He may preach acceptably and even better than many priests can do, but . . . we suffer from too much preaching and from mediocre preaching . . . The pulpit would double its efficiency if it halved its output . . . and became the business of well-trained and specially instructed men. (16 September 1921)

The Lambeth Conference 1930

The debate on voluntary clergy at the Lambeth Conference of 1930 owed its origins in part to an Anglican priest, Roland Allen (1868–1947). In his books (*Missionary Methods – St Paul's or Ours?*, Library of Historical Theology, London, 1911; *Voluntary Clergy*, 1923; and *The Case for Voluntary Clergy*, Eyre and Spottiswoode, 1930), Allen drew a sharp contrast between vocation and ministry in apostolic and his own times. The apostles sought out people who were mature in age and in faith; the Church of his day sought the young and immature. The apostles looked for fulfilment; the present Church for promise. The apostles called Christians of some standing within their local churches; the present Church recruited for a profession. In the mission field, where Christians were scattered in little groups, such a man lived before their eyes. He was of mature age and moral character, the head of a family with some position in the community. The Church needed voluntary clergy to put Baptism and the Lord's Supper where Christ and the apostles put them, at the centre of its life. A Church which relied on Lay Readers was an inadequate model of Church.

The Lambeth Bishops rejected a proposal for voluntary clergy (Resolution, Section V, 65), but the second part of the same resolution proved of great importance to Readers:

> Further, in order to meet the present pressing need, the Conference would not question the action of any Bishop who, with the sanction of the national, regional or provincial Church concerned, should authorize such licensed Reader as he shall approve to administer the chalice at the request of the parish priest.

Within two years of the Lambeth Conference a further report (*The Permanent Diaconate and 'Voluntary Clergy'*, no. 587) was received by the Convocation of Canterbury. It followed the lead of the Lambeth Bishops and recommended much greater use 'of the help which could be rendered by laymen of "mature age" and "assured position" who were "respected by their fellows", had pastoral and prophetic gifts, but who had not received a call to Holy Orders'. Such men might be given authority to administer the chalice in accordance with regulations made by the bishop of the diocese. In all the discussions on voluntary clergy there was an assumption that some would be drawn from among Readers, particularly the better educated diocesan Readers. They had also to reckon on a reluctance among some Readers *to compromise the specifically lay character of their ministry*. As for the administration of the chalice, that was another matter entirely.

The administration of the chalice

As early as 1894 it had been suggested in the Convocation of York that laity might help to administer the cup at festivals. Ten years later Bishop Yeatman-Biggs foresaw that the time might come when Readers were called upon to do this. But at the London Diocesan Conference in May 1914 the Bishop of London asked whether they were quite sure that laymen wished to receive Holy Communion on Sunday from a brother layman whom they would meet in business on Monday. Even so the item appeared on the agenda of the Annual Conference for Readers' Work in 1918. Undoubtedly the shortage of clergy during and after World War I, and the growth in the numbers of communicants, increased the need for some help with the administration of Communion.

Following the encouragement given by the 1930 Lambeth Conference, the matter was discussed by the Central Readers' Board (CRB). Administration of the cup by a person not in Holy Orders was not a question of Church order or of doctrine, but of propriety, and it was quite justified in the prevailing circumstances. But who should be allowed to administer? Age, experience, education and spirituality must all be considered. General education, even of a high standard, was not sufficient, for it had no necessary connection with religion, Christianity or Church teaching. Suitability for administering the cup was different from that of being a Reader or a preacher. Women laity would object. What if Lay Readers could administer, but not deaconesses? Some parishes would be less inclined to make sacrifices to pay an assistant priest if permission was given to Readers. Some Readers themselves were not anxious to have permission.

Five years later it was reported in the Convocation of York that there was growing resentment in many quarters against the needless intrusion of Lay Readers into the services of the Church. The administration of the cup by Readers would reduce in some degree the great Communion Service. It was left to Canon Bullard, a stalwart supporter of Readers and a member of CRB, to point out that experiments had been going on for the last seventy years in the direction of getting more help from the laity in the services of the Church.

Permission to administer the chalice was finally included in the 1941 Regulations when war again demanded change. Practice lagged behind regulations, since by 1948 at least a quarter of the dioceses had failed to give their Readers permission. The matter was raised once more, this time in Church Assembly in 1959, when it was suggested that the bishop should give special authority to Readers for certain occasions. It was a nonsense to allow a Reader to administer the cup on Easter Sunday but not on Low Sunday. The duties of Readers should not vary between dioceses, but be the same throughout the Provinces of Canterbury and York.

Readers and banns of marriage

Another challenge to Reader ministry was triggered by the banns of marriage issue. Since 1914 Readers had from time to time called the banns in the absence of the clergy, particularly in emergencies. If a Reader was taking the main service of the day and banns needed to be called, it seemed common sense for the Reader to do so, especially during the uncertainties of wartime, and afterwards too, when delay might have caused great inconvenience to the couples concerned.

A survey of dioceses carried out by CRB in 1931 reflected a confusing variety of practices among the dioceses which replied. In Bristol, Carlisle, Chichester, Peterborough, Southwark and Wakefield it was definitely not authorized. Canterbury did not authorize it but implied that it happened. In Birmingham, Chelmsford, Chester, Guildford, Lincoln and Llandaff it was neither authorized nor prohibited. Other dioceses qualified their permission. In Coventry, Hereford, Newcastle and Winchester it was permitted only in sheer necessity; in Durham, Oxford, Ripon and Truro in an emergency with the written consent of the incumbent. In Bangor and Monmouth the bishop had to give his permission beforehand, and in Rochester and St Albans, he had to be notified. Other dioceses were even more specific. In Blackburn, Bradford, and Leicester banns could be published provided the Reader signed his name in the book and added 'Licensed Reader'; in Liverpool and Sheffield, notices had to be posted on the church door. What was happening in the eighteen dioceses which did not respond to the questionnaire? Did the authorities know what was happening, or did they prefer not to know, at least as far as a public response was concerned?

These diverse responses illustrate the uncertainty and confusion in the dioceses. Some bishops put the responsibility on their legal officers; others were more sensitive to pastoral needs. The general picture also reflects how the work of Readers was developing. It was not that they sought to seize more power for themselves, nor were they trying to compete with the clergy. When Readers published banns of marriage, the clergy were obviously not present. Indeed there were many occasions when the clergy requested their Readers to call the banns. But sooner or later the question had to be faced, was it legal?

In 1932 the Church Assembly had set up a Commission 'to examine the question of the Publication of Banns of Marriage, with special reference to the proposal for the Publication of Banns by Lay Readers, and to prepare such Measure as they think expedient'. The simple intention was to enable Readers to publish banns in emergencies. This was necessary because some members of the Church's Legal Board held that, according to law, Readers had no status at all. They argued that there were no such persons as Lay Readers recognized in the official ministry of the Church of England. Morning Prayer was not Morning Prayer if an officiating minister was not present, as only he could give absolution. Therefore all services conducted by Readers were illegal. If banns had been illegally called then some marriages might not be recognized in law. Children might be illegitimate and wills (especially those relating to property!) might be called in question. In deciding to test the legality of Readers on the grounds of banns of marriage the lawyers had chosen well. They were to have a field day!

Dr John Murray, Organizing Secretary of CRB, set out the issues very clearly in June 1932. Seeing that CRB, which had been created by the 1921 Regulations, was affiliated to Church Assembly, there could be no doubt that the Church of England had accepted the revival of the office of Reader. Murray recommended that the Church should sanction a special Form of Service for the Admission of a Reader, and apply for leave to incorporate it in the Ordinal of the Book of Common Prayer; that the Rubrics or instructions should leave no doubt that the Reader was authorized to take part in the public services of the Church; and that the approval of Church Assembly and Convocation should be formally given. It was inconceivable, thought Dr Murray, that Parliament would refuse to endorse such an Act of Church Assembly.

In the debates in Church Assembly it was recognized that Readers would continue to publish banns unless the law specifically forbade it. The Bishop of Norwich spoke up for Readers. If they were to become a legally authorized and accredited ministry of the Church of England, a Measure was needed to make them such, not a 'side wind' from the banns of marriage issue. When the Banns of Marriage

Measure was approved by Church Assembly in 1934 the question of the legality of Readers was neatly avoided. The most important matter was the conduct of the service, not the publication of banns. Provided that the banns were published in the course of an authorized service, it was thought that 'no special or additional authority for publication of banns need be required'. The House of Bishops thus believed that 'a certain number of legal difficulties of a technical kind, though serious if raised, would thereby be avoided'. Of a Measure to give legal recognition to Readers there was no sign.

Many Readers felt a sense of grievance at the inability of those who managed the ecclesiastical system to make up their minds. It was not enough to claim that Readers deserved well of the Church, while leaving them in a twilight where they might be called upon for sacred functions, but were apparently not to be given legal recognition. CRB felt strongly that, after an experimental period of seventy years, the time had surely come when the Church could safely give legal recognition to the office of Reader, and define its functions with indisputable authority. Yet some of the speeches in Church Assembly showed that the Reader movement had still to contend with a dead weight of prejudice.

It was left to Dr Blagden, Bishop of Peterborough and Chairman of CRB, to put the position of Readers into perspective.

> Readers were commissioned by God and authorized and licensed by the authority of the Church . . . The Reader represents an offering in Word and Prayer of the lay ministry, something which not all laymen can give, but which belongs to the lay ministry as a whole. (Address to CRB, 1935)

A wider recognition

Following the debacle of the Banns of Marriage Measure, a report on *The Work and Status of Readers* (no. 625) was brought before the Convocation of Canterbury in 1938, following a similar report in York the previous year. Readers were a living illustration of the truth that to bear witness for Christ in the world was not the prerogative of the clergy. As the Regulations of 1921 were too narrow and cramping for modern conditions, they were not always observed. Hence there was a wide variation between dioceses. The purpose of the report was to provide a framework within which bishops might exercise their rightful discretion.

The report recognized that the work of Readers was not confined to taking services. In countless parishes Readers were busy in Sunday schools, catechism and preparation classes; they were responsible for clubs and guilds and societies; they were constant in their visitation of the sick – pastoral work of the highest value. In short, the Church could not well do without them. As a body, Readers represented an enrichment of the ministry of the laity without encroaching on the functions and dignity of the priesthood. Yet a lively discussion concerned where Readers were to place the alms after they had received them from the sidesmen. In Chester, where Readers were forbidden to enter the sanctuary, it was not unknown for the alms to be placed on the floor!

During World War II the duties of Readers again became a critical issue in some parishes. In 1941, Convocation codified all the Reader Regulations and gave them its full authority. On the legal side a schedule of forms was published. These included a Form of Declaration to be signed by all candidates for the Office of Reader, a Form of Certificate of Admission, and Forms of Licence for parochial and diocesan Readers including their public duties, and an authorized Office of the Admission of Readers.

In addition to the functions already permitted, the 1941 Regulations gave Readers authority to publish banns of marriage, to give addresses (except at Holy Communion), to receive the offerings of the people and place them on the credence table, and, by special permission of the bishop, to read the Epistle and to administer the cup at Holy Communion. The distinction between consecrated and unconsecrated buildings was discontinued, as 'by far the greater part of the Readers' work now consists in taking services in parish churches'. For the first time Readers' dress was mentioned in the Regulations: 'In the conduct of public worship the Reader should wear cassock, surplice, the badge of his office and the hood of his degree'. A diocesan Reader was no longer 'commissioned'; he was licensed to exercise his office in the parish of any incumbent in the diocese, whereas the parochial Reader was licensed as an assistant to the incumbent of his parish.

The 1941 Regulations also confirmed the work of Diocesan Readers' Boards, on which Readers were to be adequately represented, 'to carry out the directions of the Bishop in all matters affecting the registration, organization and work of Readers in the diocese, and in particular to supervise and encourage their studies, conferences and devotional meetings'. Similary CRB was to co-ordinate the organization of the dioceses, and to maintain and develop the work of Readers generally, under the authority of the Archbishops and Bishops.

Looking forward to its centenary, CRB put forward further recommendations in 1962, but these were not approved until 1969, when new Regulations gave Readers authority to read the Gospel and to preach at Holy Communion, to administer the paten as well as the chalice, and to present the offerings of the people rather than place them on the credence table. The adoption of the blue scarf (gradually becoming more familiar since the Archbishops' letter authorizing it in 1958) was encouraged. Most important was undoubtedly the change in Canon Law which opened the Office of Readers to women. (This significant development will be discussed more fully in Chapter 10.) It was also agreed that extensions to the duties of Readers could be authorized by the more convenient Regulations rather than by slower and more cumbersome changes in Canon Law.

Stipendiary Readers

LICENSED READER seeks post, Winton or Rochester; eleven years in present parish. Children's services, men's guilds, active habits. (Name and address given). Clapham.

This advertisement in the first volume of *The Reader and Lay Worker* in 1904 is typical of many inserted by stipendiary Readers who, often through no fault of their own, found themselves suddenly without employment. A stipendiary Reader earned his living by his Church work. At best he had heard the call of God to work amongst his fellows, and could not be content with giving less than his whole time and energy to this service. He almost certainly lacked the necessary qualifications for the priesthood. He did all that voluntary Readers could do, together with much pastoral work, especially visiting.

In parishes where men of leisure are few or non-existent, it is not unknown for the stipendiary Reader to be Scoutmaster, Club Leader, Sunday School Superintendent, Organist and Choirmaster all at the same time. (*Church Family Newspaper*, 20 July 1923)

Like the voluntary Reader the stipendiary had no security of tenure. The removal or death of the incumbent or even a clash of personalities or policies might enforce dismissal or a change of job at very short notice. Poorer parishes in particular employed them because they were very much cheaper, and usually more mature and less trouble, than curates. From time to time their plight was taken up in Convocation and CRB, but no effective action was taken until the mid-1930s.

As early as 1914 the *Church Times* deplored the unthinking way the dioceses had treated stipendiary Readers, in an article entitled *Ruined Readers*.

> The qualifications required, the status of the men employed, the scope of functions entrusted to them, their tenure of office, the stipends they receive while at work, and the provisions made for them when their working days are over, are matters which have been left to adjust themselves . . . there are no rules at all . . . His pay is a pittance which, if some men can afford to take, no Church can afford, for its own credit, to offer . . . The Church had invited them to enter its service and must not practise that sin of sweating labour which it denounces vigorously enough in secular life.

In 1914 most stipendiary Readers were earning between £60 and £80 per annum, and their lives were a long struggle with poverty and hardship. What this might mean for the individual was graphcally described by Thomas Bilsborough in a letter in *The Lay Reader* (vol. xviii, April 1921). Bilsborough was a diocesan Reader, but he had 51 years of service to the Church behind him, and was a founder member of the Ripon Readers' Benevolent Association.

Scrapped at 60. Mr James Moore was for 16 years Lay Reader at the Cathedral Church, Sheffield, then became the lay minister of a new parish. For 25 years this gentleman toiled at ill-paid and ill-appreciated work, but when the parish was legally formed a fledgling curate was brought in, and the white-haired, kindly old shepherd was sacked. A subscription list, aspiring to a modest £250, raised £93–5s., then died . . . The last seen of this old man, bled white by a rich Church, was his pathetic figure in a Labour Exchange queue, seeking a job.

Bilsborough then asked what the Sheffield Lay Readers' Association had to say, but if any action was taken none was reported in *The Lay Reader* for the rest of the year. Why could not Readers care for their old and poor brethren 'equally as well as our Wesley brethren did'?

Despite the voices raised on their behalf, and the provisions made by some bishops, stipendiary Readers continued to be employed in 'a horrible form of cheap labour', as it was called in Convocation. In 1935, however, CRB set up a Stipendiary Readers' Committee to administer a Fund for their relief. Of the 429 known stipendiary Readers, more than half worked for various societies like the Church Army and the Missions to Seamen. Half the stipendiary Readers were aged between 40 and 70 but four, who were training to become deacons, were under 30. It was known that some former Church Army Readers, who had been deemed unsuitable for the work, had become independent stipendiary Readers; one earned the reputation of an habitual beggar. Much of the work of the Stipendiary Readers' Committee was concerned with individual cases of poverty, infirmity, and unforeseen expenses including sickness bills. In one case at least, an immediate grant of £10 was made to prevent action by bailiffs.

The life of CRB's Stipendiary Readers' Fund may be divided into three phases. In the first phase, from 1935 to 1947, just under £1,000 was raised and 22 urgent cases dealt with. In the second phase, the 'One-third Scheme' came into operation. If after a means test income fell short of an agreed 'ceiling', the difference was made up by equal contributions from the employing diocese, Central Board of Finance and the Readers' Stipendiary Fund. Over £4,000 was raised for the Fund during this period, with contributions mainly from dioceses. In the final phase, from 1960 to 1976, the Church of England Pensions Board included stipendiary Readers in the pension scheme and took over the Central Board of Finance's share. The Readers' Stipendiary Fund continued to raise money – almost £6,000 – until the Fund was closed at the Annual General Meeting in March 1976. Only three beneficiaries remained, aged 97, 88 and 84, and no new applications had been received for ten years.

Under Canon E6 (4) 1969, no further stipendiaries were to be licensed without proper arrangements for pensions and insurance against accident and sickness. Stipendiary Readers had more or less worked themselves out of the system.

It would be unfair to stipendiary Readers to give the impression that all was centred on their appalling conditions of service. As an example of stipendiary Readers, Mr William Shaw of Runcorn, whose retirement was noted in *The Runcorn Guardian*, deserves mention. Born in 1841 in Worcestershire, he worked on the canals before joining the Royal Navy and travelling world wide, and then coming ashore to serve as a Liverpool policeman for ten years. During this time he became attached to a church in Toxteth, trained as a Reader, and in 1878 joined the Mersey Mission to Seamen. For 46 years he served the Mission in Runcorn, raising funds for the Mission church and schoolroom, and providing a Seamen's Institute where all were welcomed. 'His enthusiasm for the work and the appealing nature of his personality have undoubtedly been the principal factors in making the local station of the Mission a history of successes . . . The best wishes of the neighbourhood will go with him irrespective of party, class or creed.' High praise indeed in 1922!

Why did the office of Reader survive?

By its centenary in 1966, the office of Reader had become well established in the life of the Church, though it was still not fully accepted everywhere. The decline in the numbers of the clergy meant that opportunities for Readers increased, as did the demands made upon them, not only in church but in the pastoral, educational and general life of the parish. Despite the arguments for sub-deacons or a permanent diaconate, the existence of an active *lay* ministry was a gift which the Church squandered at its peril.

Why then did Readers survive? From the beginning they included middle- and upper-class, well educated, articulate gentlemen, often related to those in high places in both Church and State. They gave their time and their energy in the service of the gospel and of the Church. As diocesan Readers, their ministry was acceptable to clergy and laity alike in a number of parishes. Within the dioceses, however, they met together with the less well educated (though not necessarily less intelligent) parochial Readers to share common concerns of ministry and faith, training opportunities and devotional meetings. Both diocesan and parochial Readers were men who could speak for themselves and for the brotherhood, often from a very intimate knowledge of Church life within and beyond parish boundaries.

The strength of Reader ministry was from time to time a source of conflict. As we have seen, Readers were sometimes the focus of mistrust and resentment from both laity and clergy. At holiday times and in emergencies people were thankful to have a Reader at hand, and while some obviously aped the clergy, most resisted appeals to consider themselves as possible permanent deacons or sub-deacons. While 'only the Reader' became in some quarters a signal to stay away from church, Readers in general had moved on from a stop-gap ministry to a lay ministry in its own right, working in partnership with clergy and laity in the service of God.

4: Selection and Initial Training

Education in the Church
At the beginning of the nineteenth century a 'good education' and a recommendation to the bishop were sufficient qualification for ordination to the ministry of the Church of England. But by the middle of Victoria's reign about a quarter of the clergy were non-graduate (Owen Chadwick, *The Victorian Church*, vol. 2, A. & C. Black 1972, p. 247). These tended to be drawn from the middle rather than the upper classes, and received their theological education from the new theological colleges. Some of these were founded by independently funded private trusts, to reflect the distinctive teaching of evangelical, Anglo-Catholic or broad Church parties. Sometimes situated in rural areas or cathedral cities, they provided a residential training in quasi-monastic communities with a regular discipline of worship and private prayer, and an academic study of theology.

More important for recent Reader training has been the development in various parts of the country of theological courses for part-time non-residential candidates, married or single, women and men, for ordained ministry. The first of these was the Southwark Ordination Course, founded in 1960. Intended at first to provide for Non-Stipendiary Ministers, that is those who continue with their secular employment or who take early retirement and are self-supporting, the Courses also train some candidates for the full-time ministry. Their students go through the same selection procedures, and their training is assessed in the same way, and at the same standards, as those in residential colleges.

Some people believe that these Courses have an advantage over the residential colleges in that they seek to encourage ministerial formation and disciplined habits of prayer and spirituality within, rather than isolated from, the pressures of normal Christian life. Furthermore, because they are *local* courses, they have the great merit of training together people of different ecclesiastical backgrounds. This is a model which commends itself to many of those responsible for Reader training in the dioceses, though obviously in a less intensive format.

In the wider scene of education in the Church, week by week, regular congregations grow in faith through the liturgy and through a regular diet of – usually brief – sermons. Religious publishing flourishes as never before and outstanding religious programmes on radio and television prove very popular, reaching a wider audience, many of whom have no links with the Church. Spring Harvest attracts thousands of all ages who gather annually for study and inspiration. Thousands more take part in house groups, especially in Lent when they often join with Christians of other denominations. In 1983 over 12,000 people committed themselves to Christian study courses lasting at least one year (Rhoda Hiscox, *Eager to Learn*, ACCM, 1986, p. 4).

Many dioceses have their own conference centres which are booked up at weekends a year ahead by different Church groups willing to pray, work, talk and share together on a variety of topics. The retreat movement continues to grow in popularity and to attract people from all wings of the Church, as do societies representing almost every aspect of Christian life. Most dioceses have full- or part-time Adult Education Officers or Directors of Ministry or Training.

The selection of Readers

It is against this background that the selection and training of Readers must be considered. The early Readers were not so much 'selected' as already there, continuing work which they had already been doing. By 1884 three simple criteria for the selection of Readers were set out in the Diocese of Llandaff: they had to be examined, 'the same for all classes of person', be fairly acquainted with the elements of Christian doctrine and 'able to teach without any disaster to the Church'.

By June 1914, correspondents in the *Church Family Newspaper* reflect a wide range of attitudes towards the selection of Readers. Clergy were afraid to use Readers lest the laity thought they were slacking. The laity resented the ministry of other laity. The Honorary Secretary of Southwark Readers condemned the failure of the clergy to see in their laymen immense possibilities for reaching outsiders. One would-be Reader nominated by his incumbent heard nothing more for eighteen months. By 1921 the Annual Conference on Readers' Work was asking whether the intellectual and theological qualifications of Readers should be raised to a higher level, with uniform standards in all dioceses. This is the first indication of the need for *national* selection criteria.

The importance of a uniform standard for parochial stipendiary Readers and a general standard of education for all Readers was acknowledged though not achieved. In 1938, the report on *The Work and Status of Readers* (Convocation of Canterbury, no. 625) spoke of selection and training as 'not haphazard or slapdash' (pointers to what had been discovered, perhaps?), but by character, ability, devout churchmanship and sense of vocation, a person would be recognized as fit for Readers' work. This report recommended that, before admission, a potential Reader's knowledge of the faith should be adequately tested, and careful instruction given in the art of reading and the main principles of elocution and voice production. In some places recruits were expected to 'give their witness in their daily lives in the fields and in the factories, in the office and in the school, in the pits and in the workshops'.

During the last fifty years changes in society and in the Church, together with much higher standards of education, have been reflected in the nature of the ministry Readers exercise. Since a major part of the ministry of Readers lies in preaching and teaching, they must be able to acquire a theological foundation and develop skills of communication. Some dioceses have developed prevocational courses in which participants explore various kinds of ministry, ordained and lay. Others provide basic adult education programmes leading into training for Readers and for those more interested in authorized pastoral work. The selection procedure might well consist of a single interview with the Warden in some dioceses, while others insist on a series of interviews or even a whole day's selection workshop.

In view of this diversity, the report of a Wardens' Working Group, *The Ministry and Training of Readers in the Church of England* (1986), recommended that Central Readers' Conference should draw up guidelines to assist dioceses to devise their own framework for selection for Reader ministry. A Working Party was set up, and its report is considered in Chapter 15. The challenge, in the present as in the past, is to ensure that potential Readers are encouraged to discover and explore their gifts in the service of the kingdom of God.

Initial training

'It will be a great day for the Church of England when she realizes the importance and sets herself whole-heartedly to evolve and train the Ministry of her laymen' remarked a speaker at the tenth anniversary meeting of the Central Readers' Board in 1932. Although training appeared almost every year as an item on the agenda of CRB, there was no national scheme of training until the Common Entrance Examination (CEE) was instituted in 1946.

The road to establish even basic standards was long and hard. In Manchester, attention had to be given to the needs of weaker candidates, with a plea for plain and definite examination questions and for allowances for bad spelling and poor grammar. Even when candidates knew there was an examination and were willing to sit it, they sometimes did not buy the necessary books and even forgot the day and time of the examination. In London, preparation took up two evenings a week for twelve weeks, with no exemptions except for people with theological qualifications. Courses of study normally included a general knowledge of the Bible, the life and teaching of Jesus, and the Book of Common Prayer and its doctrine as expressed in the Catechism. The real difficulty then, and some would say now, was 'getting people to think'.

In 1948 the first CEE took place. Alongside the central examination, the dioceses retained responsibility for testing the Reader's ability in reading, speaking, teaching, catechizing and preaching. Of the two candidates, one failed and one passed. The examination soon became more widely accepted, if not more popular, though educational standards remained a problem with approximately a two-thirds pass rate. In 1951 the course was renamed the General Readers' Examination (GRE) and the number of candidates rose to 80. By 1956, eighteen dioceses participated, including the diocese of Mashonaland. Some dioceses, however, were only entering their strong candidates and admitting their weaker ones on their own test.

The standards of both preparation and examinations were a cause of great concern. There was 'a woeful ignorance of the New Testament', with nearly half the entrants failing, but 'fewer really bad howlers'. Answers on the Book of Daniel which accurately described the lions' den and said nothing else would not earn a pass mark; on the other hand examiners looked out for alert and lively minds and occasionally discerned them. Some dioceses, however, remained convinced that General Readers' Examination was unsuitable for their conditions.

In 1968 the GRE underwent a major revision and for the first time a small committee reported to CRB. Congregations were better educated than in the past, so the Reader must show clear evidence of an adequate basic knowledge of the faith and practice of the Church, and be able to expound them intelligently and intelligibly. The examination was to consist of four papers, each of three hours, on the Bible, Church History, Christian Worship and Church Doctrine, with two extended studies, on the Bible (Part II) and the

Ministry of the Word, to be written at home. Older candidates might be excused the examination, but would study the five subjects and write six papers at home. These candidates, provided they satisfied the examinations in all six papers, would not qualify for GRE certificates, but their dioceses would be assured that they had the necessary knowledge and ability to fit them for Reader ministry.

An Examinations Committee was set up to work the scheme, prepare regulations, set and mark the examinations and issue guidelines and book lists for candidates. Within five years the number of candidates had more than doubled and the success rate had risen to about 80 per cent. But searching questions continued to be asked, not least by some tutors and Wardens. Was the training of Readers best carried out by examinations and by cramming? Might not lessons be learned from adult education provided by Local Education Authorities, or by commercial firms? Should training in visiting, especially hospital visiting, be included?

The General Readers' Certificate

In 1975 another new scheme for training Readers was launched, influenced indirectly by general educational trends. An examinations system was not considered the best way to measure the gifts and understanding of mature and responsible Christians in relation to the variety of tasks associated with the practice of Reader ministry. Examinations were abandoned in favour of an essay scheme assessed both centrally, and locally in the dioceses. In a paper entitled *Suggestions for Tutors* (July 1975), the aim of the course material was set out in knowledge-centred terms, together with an indication of an adequate coverage of the area of study concerned, notes to guide the candidate, and suggestions for reading.

The material consisted of four booklets, entitled: A *Biblical Foundations*; B *The Christian Tradition*; C *The Christian Present*; and D *The Work of a Reader*. Each booklet contained a list of topics, supplemented by a paragraph of notes on each one, and a book list of eight or more pages. The booklets have been updated from time to time. Section A now includes 67 topics; B, 42 topics; C, 49 topics. Section D is more practically based, relating the formation of Readers to their local communities and congregations. While neither tutor nor candidate need be put off by the apparent bulk of the material provided, the present *Guide to Candidates* clearly states that every candidate will know something, 'if only two or three sentences', about all these topics, to obtain 'an idea of the total shape of biblical, historical and contemporary theology, ethics and spirituality'. After being assessed in the dioceses, sixteen essays (four for each section) are submitted to Central Readers' Conference for external assessment. Successful candidates are awarded the General Readers' Certificate.

In 1975 the hope was that the Reader would gain a new understanding of what it means, for example,

> to accept an historic faith in an historical setting, to discover the contemporary relevance of the great biblical themes, to sense the liveliness of it all – and to see himself [women were admitted in 1969!] as a Reader in the midst of it all.

There was no intention of being 'too academic'. It was hoped that tutors, clerical or lay, would stand alongside the candidates, guiding, exploring and spreading out the material. External assessors would discern whether candidates had developed a feel for the subject, could use the knowledge they had accumulated, think with some degree of clarity, exercise some degree of judgement, and express themselves clearly and reasonably intelligently on the subject.

In an article in *Theology* (vol. lxxviii, no. 62, August 1975), the Rev. Robert Morgan introduced the new scheme, which he hoped might become a model for training laity in general. He envisaged Reader training encouraging interaction between Christians academically trained in theology, and Christians with a variety of skills in a very complex world, leading to a cross-fertilization which would enrich both society and Church.

There is no doubt that under the Rev. Bryant Crane (Director of Studies until December 1989) and his team of moderators, standards of Reader training improved enormously. Consequently the respect for Readers has also increased among many congregations and clergy. The course set national standards while providing flexibility for dioceses and individual candidates. It enabled people to lay the foundations of theological study and at the same time provided a possible framework for a lifetime's reading. But questions must be asked.

Had the course-makers called upon the pool of sophisticated educational expertise to be found among Readers themselves, the programme might have been very different. The scheme reflected no underlying educational philosophy, no understanding of curriculum development, no awareness of how adults learn, no idea of building on the gifts, skills and expertise which Readers in training bring with them. The booklets failed to distinguish between initial and post-admission training and provided a collection of questions rather than a progressive scheme of work. More seriously, *the programme did not encourage Readers to apply their theological studies, to ask their own questions, or to relate one section of their study to the others.*

Despite the example of the Open University and other distance-learning schemes, the presentation of the material was, and still is, dreary and unhelpful to the learners. It is not surprising that only a quarter of candidates admitted to the office of Reader in recent years have obtained the General Readers' Certificate.

Some dioceses have developed their own initial schemes of training which take account of a wider range of learning methods, develop the tools of theological study through the handling of key topics, and encourage a more practical relationship between training and ministry than that achieved by writing sixteen essays for external assessment. The Wardens' report of 1986 on *The Ministry and Training of Readers in the Church of England* recommended a new approach to Reader training which resulted in ACCM's Committee for Theological Education setting up a Working Party in 1989. Its report, which recommended phasing out the General Readers' Certificate, is considered in Chapter 15.

5: Reader Education After Admission

Training after admission

The admission and licensing of Readers marked, and still marks, only the end of the beginning. Many dioceses encouraged further training, often at first in the form of recommended study books which were discussed at local or diocesan gatherings. Most Readers received their post-admission training on the job, and much depended on the interest, skill and sensitivity of the incumbent.

The possibilities were well set out in an article in the *Church Family Newspaper* (27 June 1923). Incumbents were advised to draw up a monthly list of duties, to be discussed with the Reader both before and afterwards, with words of encouragement and warning as appropriate. One of the clergy or an experienced worker should take the new Reader to a service, giving him a modest share of the work, which could be talked over on the way home. Where his work was strong, he should be given a first-rate book so that he might go from strength to strength. Where it was weak, he should be given an elementary book, and work alongside another 'so that precept and example shall unite with the willing mind to strengthen and improve that side of the work'.

Proposals for further examination found little favour among Readers whose ministry was additional to full-time employment. Readers were urged to continue their studies, and Diocesan Readers' Boards to see that they were continued, but neither received much help or encouragement. In 1933, however, Central Readers' Board sponsored what became known as Continuation Courses, three progressive courses of reading under guidance, to encourage habits of learning and a broader outlook by extending Readers' understanding of basic aspects of the faith. At first, either the examinations were too difficult or the candidates badly prepared and the results were discouraging for all. Readers were encouraged to take one course at a time, and to undertake at least one or two years' study before the examination.

Some idea of the content may be obtained from the 1944 syllabus. The First Course consisted of one of the Synoptic Gospels, The

Prophets of the Eighth Century BC, Early Church History to AD 461, and Doctrine, based on the Creeds. For the Second Course, Readers studied The History of the Old Testament, The Pauline Epistles, English Church History and Christian Evidences. The Third Course covered The Wisdom Literature, The Johannine Writings, The Applications of Christian Principles to Life, A Special Period of Church History, Philosophy of Religion and Comparative Religions.

With such an ambitious programme of study, by 1969 a significant number of Readers were asking for copies of the syllabus as guides for private study with no intention of taking the examinations. A review of the pass lists for 1957–67 shows that the annual number of successful candidates for the first courses varied between nineteen and three; for the second course, fourteen and four; for the third course nine and two. With about 7,000 licensed Readers, it was obvious that these courses were not meeting the needs of those for whom they were intended.

These Continuation Courses were superseded in the early 1970s by a series of annual study guides of a more practical nature. For example, the course for 1971–72, entitled 'Preacher, Pulpit and People', was written by a member of CRB, Dr Hugh Fearn. Its eight sections were brief but thought-provoking, containing much practical advice, and questions for discussion. I cannot resist quoting the final one: 'Throw away your sermon notes. Is this good advice?'

Other forms of post-admission training depended on diocesan initiatives. Most dioceses have an annual conference or study day, about half have some kind of weekend course, and a quarter have an annual retreat. These are often supplemented by area or deanery meetings. Other courses, arranged by Readers or other agencies, are available in most dioceses. The College of Preachers, the Royal School of Church Music, Hospital Chaplains and local Adult Education classes have been among those who have co-operated in Reader training.

Post-admission training has frequently involved a long, hard slog, often with disappointing results for many Readers. Perhaps Readers of Leicester fared much better 30 years earlier, when a Readers' School was held on three successive evenings at a cost of £40. The men were bused in from 40 miles away, taught, fed and sent back again to their own doors each evening. The timetable seemed quite strenuous after a day's work: 7.30, lecture; 8.15, discussion; 9.00, reporting back, followed by a good supper and the journey home.

The Archbishop's Diploma for Readers

Another form of continuation course was the Archbishops' Diploma for Readers (A.Dip.R). The first examinations took place in 1933, on a syllabus agreed by the Archbishops of Canterbury, York and Wales. The Diploma has never proved very popular, despite successive revisions.

In 1971, for example, the Diploma was awarded on the basis of 30 essays. Ten subjects had to be chosen, including at least one from each of five groups: Bible, Doctrine, Worship, Church History and Social Education. A candidate who chose the subject 'The Nature of God' in the Doctrine group, had to choose three essays from the following topics:

1. Is the Bible the 'Word of God' or 'man's word about God'? In what ways does our understanding of the Bible affect our understanding of God?
2. What does the Christian mean when he speaks of God as Creator?
3. What are the objections to a personal God and how can they be answered?
4. How can we speak of God today?
5. The God of Love and Evil in Creation.
6. 'God was in Christ reconciling the world to himself.' How can this be presented meaningfully to contemporary men?

More recently the regulations for the Diploma have again been revised on the basis of the General Readers' Certificate Course. The regulations, in force until 1990, described the Archbishops' Diploma as 'one form of continuing training, designed to bear comparison with other academic diplomas, and to encourage the development of lay theologians in the Church'. Eight essays of between 3,500 and 4,000 words, written on different topics from those submitted for the General Readers' Certificate, are required. Four essays, including one on the Gospels and one on the Epistles, must be chosen from Biblical Foundations, two from The Christian Tradition, and two from The Christian Present. In addition a short dissertation of 10,000 to 15,000 words is required, on a subject of the candidate's own choice, but approved by the Director of Studies. The subject must be related either to understanding and communicating the Christian faith today, or to a topic from within the Christian tradition or exploring the theological implications of the Reader's own work and experience. Between 1970 and 1983, 28 Diplomas were awarded.

To one who has firmly believed for some time that the education of the clergy is far too important to be left to the clergy, various proposals over many years for the Archbishops' Diploma clearly show what happens when the laity are excluded – however unintentionally – from taking responsibility for their own learning. Despite high expectations, the Diploma has never fulfilled its purpose.

Summer Refresher Courses and 'Selwyn'

One of the earliest and most significant ventures in the post-admission training of Readers began in 1881 with the first summer Refresher Course held at Keble College in Oxford. At first the courses alternated between Keble and Selwyn College, Cambridge, with occasional visits to St Augustine's, Canterbury. Since the 1930s Selwyn has been their home. The first course lasted a month, with Readers coming for as long as they were able, but with increasing costs, counter-attractions and other responsibilities, the course now takes place for eight days early in August. As early as 1883, 29 students were in residence at the first Selwyn. The numbers steadily grew, and for the last fifty years or so have varied between 80 and 100.

The pattern of the Refresher Courses was set from the beginning: a disciplined framework of worship, lectures and time for mutual edification and support. A typical day began at 7.30 a.m. in time for Mattins, short address and silent prayer. Lectures at 9.30 and 11.30 a.m. were followed by the Litany on Wednesdays and Fridays with the afternoon for walking and sightseeing. Evensong at 5.30 p.m. preceded 'Conference' for an hour or more before supper. In 1883 the 'Conferences' included Children's Services, Training the Elder Lads, Temperance Work, Sick Visiting, Scepticism, The Church and Purity, Working Men and the Church. After supper at 8.00 p.m. there was optional Bible Reading led by one of the lecturers and Compline at 10.00 p.m. The late evening was also a time for private reading, conversation with the Principal, or optional Greek New Testament for those who had the inclination and stamina.

In 1885 the programme included lectures on the Book of Common Prayer; Daniel; the Old Testament and New Testament with specific reference to morality; discussions on the Salvation Army, and a description of the Moabite Stone. There was usually a Quiet Day, often led by a visiting clergyman. By the 1950s the programme was still much the same, except that Holy Communion was preceded by Mattins at 7.15 a.m., and group discussion was introduced after Evensong. Occasionally there were lecture sessions or lighter interludes with a Brains Trust or film show after supper.

Theological themes in the 1950s and 1960s included The Christian Religion in the Age of Science (Charles Raven), The Foundation of

Real Religion (J. E. Fison), Christian Belief in God (John Burnaby), Christianity in Ethics (G. F. Woods). There was much about Anglicanism and a little about the Church in India and in Russia. There was nothing about Christianity and the professions, or Christianity in the market place. Perhaps this was because the lecturers, all of whom gave their services free of charge, were drawn entirely from the theological faculty of the University of Cambridge. There was a galaxy of speakers. Professor Owen Chadwick, Master of Selwyn from 1957, gave most generously of his own time year after year and prevailed upon his most distinguished colleagues, among them Moule, Montefiore, Lampe, Bowker, Baelz, Barrington-Ward and Cupitt, to share their learning with a most appreciative audience.

Selwyn has undoubtedly filled a very special role in the development of Reader ministry. The very first volume of *The Reader and Lay Worker* (October 1904) sets out its value:

> It was pathetic to come across some of these men at Cambridge . . . For the first time they learnt how much their ordinary life lacked. Never before had they known what it was to discuss knotty points of work with fellow workers, to pray side by side with those who felt the same needs, to find that their work, their methods, their reading and even their souls were objects of living, personal interest to genuine brothers. They go back to their work with fresh power and zeal . . .

In 1923 the *Church Family Newspaper* commented that the lectures from well-known scholars were a great help in thinking, reading and teaching for months and even years afterwards 'while the insight gained into scholarly methods of work and careful precise statement are a revelation to many and an inspiration to all.' Readers in all parts of the country and all ranks of life might find themselves confronted by very searching questions and should be prepared to meet them. One first-time student enjoyed the challenge: it was like 'having one's brains taken out, dusted, stretched and put back again'.

The continued success of the summer courses at Selwyn owed much to the vision, wisdom and drive of Dr John Murray, who attended his first Selwyn as a young lecturer in 1888, was Master of Selwyn College from 1909 to 1928, and on retirement became Honorary Secretary of CRB from 1928 to 1944. The course flourished under his leadership, teaching and friendship. A man of vision, great energy, ability and charm, Murray was quick to see the possibilities of Reader ministry and encouraged its development in every way.

The Refresher Courses had been started in 1881 by the enthusiasm and generosity of Lord Beauchamp, a prominent Reader, and with the support of Dr Frederick Temple, then Bishop of London. The Diocese of London through its Lay Helpers' Association arranged the courses until Lay Readers' Headquarters, the forerunner of CRB, took over in 1915. There was, however, one strange episode which illustrates the amateurish nature of much of Reader organization and administration. In 1950 a meeting of the Rev. James Wall, the Honorary Secretary, Captain Julian Smith, the Vice-Chairman of CRB, and two other members declared: 'Whereas Central Readers' Board is qualified to conduct courses, the Selwyn Course is a private benevolence on the part of Captain Julian Smith. In the past Central Readers' Board has merely helped him to conduct the Course. This is still technically the position. He has nominated this committee accordingly.' After this declaration of independence the minutes record with unconscious irony the forthcoming list of lectures, the first of which was 'The Forgiveness of Sins'! A separate banking account was established and Selwyn continued to be independent and self-supporting with its accounts published annually in *The Reader*.

It was left to Canon George King, who had succeeded the Rev. James Wall as Honorary Secretary, to sort out the problem in 1965 after his accidental discovery on reading through previous CRB accounts that the Selwyn courses belonged legally as well as morally to CRB. There is no doubt now that the Selwyn Committee is accountable to CRB's successor, Central Readers' Conference, to which it submits an annual report.

Though comparatively few Readers ever attended Selwyn, some of the older men attended for more than twenty years. They were attracted by the deep fellowship with other Readers, the discipline and joy of daily worship, the mental stimulation and intellectual nature of the course, and meeting and listening to theologians of international repute. For their part the university theologians were said to appreciate the opportunity of 'coming into contact with "down to earth" godliness' of the Readers, coupled with the diversity of their secular knowledge, and their experience and understanding of the Church at work in the world. The college, too, valued its link with the lay ministry of the Church of England.

Looking to the future, a 1971 report rightly stated that the association with Selwyn represented a fund of goodwill which it would be both foolish and ungrateful to lose. It suggested that the right policy, whatever variations might be made from year to year, was to continue to make the best possible use of the theological resources of Cambridge University.

Others are not so sure. While they recognize the value of Selwyn to the Readers who attend, they would want to question the present fare on offer. For example, some Readers would plead that other forms and traditions of worship, perhaps more attuned to contemporary spirituality, should be included from time to time as an alternative to the discipline of the daily offices. Valuable and stimulating as academic lectures can be, there are other ways of adult learning which are complementary, equally valid, and more suited to national rather than diocesan courses. Should Selwyn continue in its present conservative mould for another generation? Or should the link with Selwyn be preserved by exploring the resources of Cambridge and perhaps other universities in ways which are inter-disciplinary, creative, reflective and participatory, and which attract, alongside the clergy, Readers eminent in their own fields of work as course leaders and speakers?

Sometimes I dream

The selection of Readers and their initial and continuing training has grown from small and hesitant beginnings, sometimes out of desperate necessity, and sometimes because one or two people shared their vision, wisdom and enthusiasm, inspiring tutors and learners alike. Readers and the whole Church have gained from the great strides forward in Reader education. Yet these represent only a fraction of the educational opportunities which now exist for the enrichment of Readers and their wider ministry.

Sometimes I dream. I dream of a Church of England which values university faculties of theology for all the work they do in their various branches of study; which sets aside substantial funds for research projects particularly in social and pastoral theology and ethics; and which specifically encourages Readers with appropriate qualifications to engage in such research as its lay ministers. I dream of Readers taking initiatives with other Christians and with those outside the Church, exploring topics of professional interest, in, for example, the fields of medical, legal or business ethics, or engaging in radical thinking and political action in relation to issues of peace and justice and other areas of life where Christian values are threatened. I dream of Readers sufficiently competent and confident in their faith, theology and skills of communication, to work outside the institutional Church in lives of risk-taking and vulnerability. Just before waking I dream that some Readers are being welcomed as trainers of clergy in theological colleges and courses, in continuing ministerial education and in training courses for archdeacons and bishops.

6: In The Diceses

Early stages

Many of the first Readers were very isolated and did their work as best they could without encouragement and without reward, except through the responses of those to whom they ministered. As the numbers of Readers gradually increased, so did the need for some kind of regulation and organization. The early development of any form of organization for Readers at a diocesan level normally depended on the vision of the bishop, his concern for the spiritual welfare of the ever-increasing number of people in the diocese, and his encouragement of lay helpers to supplement the efforts of the clergy in mission and ministry.

In London, the diocesan Lay Helpers' Association owed its origin to a report in 1865 which argued that the laity were an integral part of the Church, 'an organic, ever-growing body'. The objects of the Association were 'first to organize, and secondly to stimulate and expand the lay religious work of the Diocese'. Members met twice a year, for a Communion service and for the Annual Meeting. By 1874 the association, which included 95 Readers and 2,150 other lay helpers, claimed to be 'as high and as low and as broad as the Church of England itself: no more, but no less'.

In Durham, Bishop Lightfoot presided over an association formed in 1881, to guide and encourage all forms of lay ministry. This association was well organized, with a strong committee including one clerical and one lay representative from every rural deanery, and the Secretary for Church Army Van Work. Local Ruri-Decanal Help Committees drew up 'Plans of Work' for Readers and probationers, important in a diocese where many mining villages were some distance from the parish church.

From these and similar beginnings the diocesan organization of Readers began to emerge. In Lincoln, for example, Readers were already at work when Bishop Edward King suggested the formation of a Guild of Lay Preachers. By 1907 the Lincoln Diocesan Association of Lay Readers was formed 'to supplement the work of the

Clergy and to add to the means used by the Church for the spiritual welfare of the people'. The Diocesan Warden had oversight of seven districts, each having its own Warden and Secretary. An Annual General meeting was held under the presidency of the bishop for united devotion and conference and for fellowship.

In London the Diocesan Readers' Board was established in 1890 with the approval of Diocesan Conference. The Board consisted of the suffragan bishops, archdeacons, four other clergy and eight laymen. Bishop F. R. Barry encouraged diocesan Readers, maintaining that their preaching in consecrated buildings was of the highest value, and that it both strengthened and supported the clergy's responsibility and position. He looked for a wider extension of Readers' liturgical duties.

In Worcester an Association of Readers was formed in 1898 to assist the clergy in various branches of parochial work. The terms of the Reader's licence were read aloud in church so that the congregation was fully aware of his duties. With the creation of the Diocese of Birmingham in 1905, Dr Yeatman-Biggs, the author of *Lay Work and the Office of Reader*, became Bishop of Worcester. He gave Readers every encouragement, and appealed for the help of the squire, the educated farmer and the professional man to assist in the ministry of the Church. In 1906 he wrote in the diocesan magazine that he was glad to make a reasonable holiday more possible for the clergy by allowing a licensed layman of position and education to conduct a service approved by him. This was expressly forbidden in Carlisle as late as 1932.

In Ripon Diocese in 1903, nine members were given grants to allow them to attend the Summer School, and clergy lectures at Ripon were open to Readers. Monthly deanery meetings were arranged, with lectures on Church History, The Book of Common Prayer, Catechizing, and Preaching for Outdoor Gatherings ('useful especially on fair grounds'). Incidentally I have often wondered whether some Readers might not be better occupied on Sunday mornings preaching at boot fairs or Sunday markets than to the converted in church!

In Llandaff, one of four Welsh dioceses, the diocesan association had been founded in 1901, though Readers had been established long before that. The situation here was complicated by the bilingual population, and rapid change to an industrial economy with new collieries and iron, steel and tinplate works. Quarterly meetings were held in different venues for 'sacred study and sweet fellowship'. Apparently 'nothing was hurried, everything being carried on decently and in order'. Llandaff normally had a small number of

Marine Readers licensed to assist the seamen's chaplain in visiting vessels and conducting services among the floating population at Cardiff, Newport, Penarth and Barry.

Development continued to be piecemeal until the 1921 Regulations proposed that every diocese should have a Board to keep a Register of Readers and to organize their work. Progress remained slow; some Boards did not come into being until the 1930s, and in Bath and Wells not until 1943. An article in the *Church Family Newspaper* (7 September 1923) suggested that some bishops were not keen: 'A level-headed Board with a wise Chairman and competent Secretary is not likely to come into conflict with the Bishop'. Some Readers' Boards had to contend with the costs of organizing conferences and problems of transport, especially in scattered dioceses. In St Asaph a Reader regularly cycled 50 miles to attend diocesan events. Though attendance might be disappointing for the organizers, the article suggested that the remedy did not lie in grumbling at the absent and calling them slackers, but in arranging smaller gatherings.

After 1922

Some fascinating glimpses of the organizations of Diocesan Readers' Boards (DRBs) are given by W. S. Williams in his *History of the Reader Movement* (1932). Williams was Honorary Secretary of London Readers' Board and also a member of Central Readers' Board. He shows that at first bishops and other members of the ecclesiastical hierarchy took an active part in DRBs. The imbalance between clergy and Readers is striking, with few Reader representatives, and almost all of them appointed by bishops. Wakefield was exceptional in electing all its Reader members. Although the clergy remained in control of DRBs, Readers like W. S. Williams (London), John Millward (Southwell, and later Derby), and Thomas Bilsborough (Ripon), made outstanding contributions to the development of the organization of Readers, both in their dioceses and nationally.

Williams gives a few clues to the life of Readers in their respective dioceses. In Exeter, a committee was set up in 1924 to consider 'how best to improve the spirituality, efficiency and numbers of Readers in the diocese'. In Leicester in addition to a monthly corporate Communion, there were meetings and lectures, a New Year's supper for Readers and their wives and an outing in the summer, to provide for the spiritual and mental equipment of Readers and the development of the social side. Oxford regulations not surprisingly provided for further study.

Regular reading must be looked upon as a definite duty, and

Readers should regard themselves as under an obligation to read the books suggested for study. It is of the first importance that all study should be based upon a careful reading of the text itself of the Bible, and not limited to text books about the Bible.

My guess is that most Readers in training in recent times will have heard similar comments from their tutors!

In Truro it was part of the Reader's duty 'to converse with persons in order to explain the doctrines and discipline of the Church, and to free the Gospel of Christ from misrepresentation and prejudice'. Exeter rejoiced in a growing number of younger men; St Albans was looking for them in 1928 when the average age of its Readers was then 55. Most Readers were expected to send in an annual return of their activities, and in some dioceses the renewal of their licenses depended on these being satisfactory.

A typical Diocesan Readers' Board

To illustrate the work of DRBs, I have taken the Diocese of Rochester as my example. It is a relatively compact diocese with a good mix of urban and rural communities.

The Minute Book of the Rochester Diocesan Order of Lay Readers begins in 1907, soon after the Diocese of Southwark was formed out of Rochester diocese. The first meeting was held not in Rochester but Westminster, with the Bishop, five clergy and four laymen present. Unlike Exeter, where according to the Minute Book the newly constituted Board met only nine times between 1925 and 1941, the Rochester records are continuous, with regular meetings since its inception. The main themes of the meetings are common to most dioceses: licensing and movements of Readers, arrangements for conferences, study books, training, Readers' regulations, finance, uniform and miscellaneous items.

Apart from recording changes of officers, there were only two references to the composition of the Board itself. In 1929, as the committee's term of office had expired, three members were nominated by the Bishop and six elected by the Conference for a period of three years. In 1942 Bishop Chavasse, then still relatively new in the diocese, praised the long service of Board members but suggested, with some justice as one member had not attended for three years, that it might be good for the Association if new members were sometimes chosen.

The accompanying Register of Readers dates from 1907 and records the names and addresses of Readers, with the date of admission, date of licence, where licensed, dates of endorsements and return. Many parochial Readers had their licenses transferred to diocesan licences after a probationary period. Licences were also granted for work in connection with the Deaf and Dumb Society, the Barbican Mission to Jews, the British and Foreign Bible Society, the Church Army, the Missions to Seamen, the Navy Mission, and the Royal Naval Barracks and Dockyard at Chatham. Transfers in and out of the diocese were recorded; some Readers were placed on a retired list; some were ordained; one or two lapsed; dates of deaths were noted when known.

As always, regulations have had to catch up with the work Readers have been called upon to do. In the 1930s, when discussions on banns of marriage and administering the chalice were uppermost, Rochester Readers were told that, if their movement were to prosper and receive its due recognition, they must not harm their cause by undertaking unauthorized duties.

Most of the business of the meetings concerned the organization of the two annual conferences and licensing services: a winter one based in the Cathedral and a summer one somewhere in the diocese. Conference programmes were usually based on the current study book. A paper was read, usually by a Reader, and discussion followed. In more recent years there have been talks, occasionally by an author of a study book, on a variety of topics, followed by group discussion and a plenary session. An analysis of the study books shows that until the mid-1960s, when one book only was prescribed, one of the books was always devotional or related to biblical studies, perhaps a commentary.

Study books included works by Charles Gore, H. Wheeler Robinson, William Temple, Alan Richardson, C. H. Dodd, Donald Coggan and Neville Ward, but only one classic of spirituality, *On the Imitation of Christ*. Some related to general Church life: in 1912, soon after the Edinburgh Missionary Conference, J. R. Mott's *The Decisive Hour of Christian Mission*; in 1936, the report of the *Commission on Church and State*; and in 1945, *Towards the Conversion of England*. Following World War I, recommended books were trying to make sense of the faith in a shattered world with such titles as *Have You Understood Christianity?*; *Reasons for Believing in Christianity*; or to relate faith to the world, *Christianity and Industrial Problems*.

Following World War II, the titles are much more inward-looking and Church-centred. In the year that Heawood's *The Humanist–Christian Frontier* was recommended, two deaneries requested books of a more practical nature. Their reaction to the book chosen for the following year, Teilhard de Chardin's *Le Milieu Divin*, is not recorded! There is little to indicate a willingness to wrestle with informed Christian thinking in relation to the world where most Readers spend most of their time. Perhaps those books, despite a small subsidy which is still given, were and are more expensive, more demanding, and more limited in appeal.

Occasionally there are hints that life among Readers was not running as smoothly as it might have done. There were the inevitable clashes between Readers and incumbents, neatly glossed over in the minutes with no names mentioned. In 1920, of 103 Readers only 29 attended the Summer Conference, despite its being 'obligatory'. No wonder the officers were sometimes exasperated!

In 1942 and again in 1968, discussions on the possibility of women Readers were met firmly with the argument that the time was not opportune. But in 1969, the year when women were admitted, in reply to a question the Warden stated that he was quite prepared to train women. To be fair to the diocese, the first women were admitted in 1970 and they now form a quarter of the Readers in the diocese. Since 1981 the Readers have chosen one woman and one man (on two occasions two women) to represent them at Central Readers' Conference.

Other initiatives have been less significant nationally, but important in the diocese. In 1935, when the legality of Readers was being questioned, a Diocesan Sunday was declared, when all Readers were given special permission to preach in parish churches. In some deaneries there are regular meetings between Readers and Methodist Local Preachers. In 1947 a Resolution was sent to CRB suggesting that secretaries of all dioceses should be informed that no Reader requesting to be transferred to a new diocese be licensed until a recommendation was received from the immediate preceding secretary. Despite CRB's concurrence, twenty years later the system was still 'found wanting'.

Readers in Rochester diocese have in the past maintained a certain independence from CRB. The first mention in the minutes in 1922 is unfriendly, to say the least: 'The Organization of Readers has been taken over by the Archbishops and Bishops and a Central Board constituted'. In 1956 the members decided not to make grants to support Readers at the Selwyn Summer School, preferring to use their surplus funds for the benefit of all Readers. In 1974 an enthusiastic and able Warden launched an enlarged syllabus of training to include the World Church, Ethics, Communication and Evangelism, with a greater use of seminars instead of lectures or private study. Preaching conferences and pastoral training days have been obligatory for many years, so that Readers are prepared for a preaching and teaching ministry within a pastoral context. Training in Rochester has remained independent of the General Readers' Certificate. Some would claim it has provided a better training from a wider base, and it is more suited to the work Readers are called to do.

Financially, Rochester had always supported CRB, but in 1972 CRB asked for a subscription of £1 per head, which would have meant an increase from £42 to £200 for the diocese. Not surprisingly, the financiers worked on CRB's accounts to show that none of its activities such as training paid for itself. Furthermore, because other dioceses were defaulting, the burden was falling on those who did pay. The strong line taken by Rochester and other dioceses, together with persistent action from CRB, meant that the situation gradually improved. Needless to say, with the appointment of a Rochester Reader, Mr C. J. Ball, as Honorary Secretary of Central Readers' Conference (as CRB became) from 1980 to 1988, relations with the centre became more supportive.

Finance

From the beginning Readers have, with few exceptions, given their services voluntarily to the Church. The exceptions included stipendiary Readers, Scripture Readers, who often worked full-time for very small rewards under the Scripture Readers Association, and those who worked for the Church Army, the Missions to Seamen and other Societies.

Looking at the financing of the work of DRBs as a whole, it is immediately apparent that there are hidden, and often considerable, subsidies. Most Wardens or Bishop's Advisers hold other appointments in parish or cathedral, or possibly as Diocesan Officers with responsibility for Readers as part of a wider brief for lay ministry or adult education. The number of lay, and normally honorary, Wardens is slowly increasing. This determines the amount of time and energy Wardens are able to give to the Reader side of their work. Some appear to manage miracles, while others are left as frustrated jugglers trying to keep an eye on everything that is going on. Administrative provision varies from a diocesan office and full access to diocesan facilities, to no help at all from the diocese and a Reader assistant secretary addressing envelopes by hand.

The credit for establishing workable financial arrangements for DRB's is generally given to Mr John Millward, a Reader in Southwell, and later Derby, and Chairman of the Finance Committee of Headquarters before the formation of CRB. The Millward Scheme, as it was called, was gradually adopted by all DRBs. Its twofold basis was very simple. First, parishes which had one or more licensed Readers were required to pay a small annual fee for each Reader. Secondly, parishes utilizing the services of Readers (other than those licensed to them) paid a fee for each Sunday morning or evening service taken. The fees were paid to the Diocesan Board, not to the Readers themselves.

There were two underlying principles to the Millward scheme. One was the need of every DRB to have the finance to carry out its own work, and to contribute to central funds. The other, that it was a bad principle for the Church that the services of Readers should be obtainable without charge while a fee had to be paid for clerical services. By the 1930s the Millward Scheme formed the basis of the financial arrangements in most dioceses, though adapted to local circumstances. The fee varied from five shillings to ten shillings and sixpence for each Sunday service. Parishes paid to the diocese an annual capitation fee varying from six to twelve shillings. Even by 1951, however, one diocesan representative reported that as far as his diocese was concerned all expenses that could be avoided, were, and that everything was done to supply a lay minister to the Church costing practically nothing!

The Millward Scheme still forms the financial basis for most DRBs, but London and Chelmsford, for example, provide for Readers as part of the whole ministry of the diocese. At the other end of the scale the Diocese of Guildford is virtually self-financing, apart from a small annual grant. Elsewhere, capitation fees vary from £5 upwards, which may or may not include a copy of *The Reader*, which dioceses are encouraged to buy in bulk.

The cost of training both before and after licensing also varies considerably from diocese to diocese. Some dioceses organize their training budgets centrally. Others fund initial training centrally, but make a small charge for in-service training events, on the practical grounds that Readers are more likely to attend if they have paid for themselves in advance! All Readers may claim travelling expenses, though not all choose to do so. As an indication of changing times, in Lincoln diocese Readers were allowed to claim twopence per mile when using a bicycle during World War II, but by 1989 car allowances had risen to 30p per mile. As in other well-organized dioceses the current regulations in Lincoln note that 'any data of a confidential nature stored on computer storage devices by any of the Association's officers shall be registered and protected under the Data Protection Act 1986, and as amended'.

There can be no doubt that some Readers' Boards are not as well organized as they might be, and that the prevailing financial arrangements with the diocese are sometimes a barometer of their life in general. The growing trend in dioceses to recognize Reader ministry as part of the whole ministry of the Church, and therefore to take financial responsibility for it, is to be welcomed. It is not that DRBs want to evade their responsibilities; they certainly do not. But just as partnership between clergy and Readers is gradually being worked out in the parish, so partnership and the sharing of human and other resources can strengthen both diocese and Readers in their shared mission in the world.

Recent developments

In some dioceses, integration of the funding of DRBs has gone hand in hand with changes in structures by which they are being drawn into Boards of Ministry or Training. It is essential that, where this happens, Readers must be represented on the appropriate board or council by Readers themselves. This also applies when sub-committees or working groups are appointed. The Church needs to hear the voice of its experienced Readers, both women and men, and Readers need to listen to the voice of the wider Church. The consequent interchange of ideas, the struggle of working together at a difficult problem, the valuing of insights, and the professional and practical expertise of every member, can only enrich the life of the Church, besides being a more responsible use of everyone's time, talents and resources. This is already happening informally.

Go through any diocesan directory and compare the membership of diocesan committees with the list of Readers, and it becomes obvious that a surprising number of Readers serve as elected members of Diocesan Synods and representatives on its committees. Sometimes there is an obvious professional connection, as with Diocesan Boards of Finance or Education; at other times Readers are there because they care and are trusted representatives, or have been co-opted for their particular understanding and concern.

With the increasing cost of travel, more meetings are being held regionally. Both Wardens and DRB Secretaries now have regional meetings in most areas of the country. The Wardens are able to share their concerns over the selection and training of Readers as well as more mundane matters. At a recent regional meeting of secretaries, the topics covered included their 'job descriptions', financial support of Readers from dioceses and parishes, and Readers and Extended Communion. Representing Central Readers' Conference, the Honorary Deputy Secretary was able to share news of the progress of various working parties. The day enabled participants to get to know their opposite numbers in neighbouring dioceses, and to share all kinds of information in ways impossible at the annual secretaries' meeting. New secretaries gained a new perspective – and new friends. Regional meetings not only build up a network of closer relationships; they also encourage a more real understanding of the underlying principles of good practice, and foster confidence.

DRBs move at different speeds according to their particular circumstances and the specific interests, gifts and expertise of their bishop, his staff, and diocesan and Reader officers. It is still true that far too many members of DRBs are reluctant to retire, and to give younger women and men an opportunity to serve. Some younger Readers are frustrated because they are unable to make their views heard either in their DRBs or centrally. As a result the whole Reader movement is the poorer.

There is another way in which DRBs might begin to serve the Church, now that the ministry of Readers has been accepted and affirmed. According to the records, DRBs seem to spend almost all their time looking inwards, or looking back over their shoulders. Perhaps the time has come when they should be looking outwards. For example, at a recent Annual General Meeting of one DRB, it was resolved to make representations to the local examinations Board concerning one item of the Religious Education syllabus for the GCSE examination. Is this the kind of action DRBs should be taking? Or should such action be taken only through Diocesan Synod or appropriate professional associations? How might Readers, as *trained and competent lay ministers* of the Church of England, begin to voice their wider corporate concerns?

7: A National Movement 1: Central Readers' Board

Before 1922

When the Archbishops issued the 1921 Regulations, there was already in existence an informal but well-organized national body, working well and self-financing. As early as the 1880s, Readers in some dioceses had begun to meet together, but the first truly inter-diocesan event was the first Summer Refresher Course held at Keble College, Oxford in 1881 (as described in Chapter 5). A core of Readers who met annually at Keble or Selwyn would have come to know one another very well, as the earliest courses lasted for three to four weeks for those who could stay for the whole time. Besides worship, lectures and study, those concerned for the development of Reader ministry would have had ample opportunity for exchanging ideas and practical information.

By 1896 the first publication for Readers was produced under the editorship of Dr John Murray. Called *Readers' Work: Notes and News for Licensed Readers*, it was published quarterly by the London Diocesan Readers' Board, and proved to be the forerunner of *The Reader and Lay Worker* (the title was soon changed to *The Lay Reader*, and eventually to *The Reader*), first published in 1904. Readers were beginning to organize themselves! The next step forward, first suggested in *The Reader and Lay Worker* in 1907, and warmly welcomed at the Keble Summer School, was the formation of a central body for Readers. The Archbishops gave their approval, and bishops were invited to nominate two representatives, one of whom should be lay. The first meeting of the Annual Conference on Readers' Work took place in 1908 under the presidency of Dr Murray.

In 1914 a small room was rented in 7 Dean's Yard, Westminster, and the Lay Readers Headquarters was established with A. W. Nott as the Honorary Secretary. Just after that, an advertisement appeared in *The Lay Reader* which described its work:

> Headquarters undertakes the publication of books and papers in the interests of the movement, purchases and forwards books to

Readers on receipt of the published price, keeps record files of licences issued throughout the Anglican Communion and the regulations of every diocese, answers queries connected with any branch of Readers' work.

Subscriptions were invited from diocesan organizations and from individuals. Those who subscribed one guinea received *The Lay Reader* monthly.

It was a programme of activities which, I suspect, challenged the resources of the staff then, and would be beyond the slender Central Readers' Conference staff of today, partly because the Reader movement is larger, and partly because some of the duties such as handling books and recording licences throughout the Anglican Communion are no longer appropriate. But promoting the Reader movement and answering queries about all aspects of the work of Readers never ceases.

At the Annual Conference on Readers' Work in 1918 there was a plea for greater efficiency, better organization, more co-ordination between dioceses, and, above all, for the fullest use to be made of existing regulations. A central organization was needed to 'act as a kind of foster-mother' to backward Diocesan Readers' Boards, with an organizing secretary who could visit them and give advice and help. Proposals for both DRBs and a Central Readers' Board were included in the 1921 Regulations. For the first time Readers were about to have a fully recognized national body.

The Central Readers' Board 1922–76
The first meeting of CRB took place on 21 November 1922, with representatives from 25 dioceses. A letter from the Archbishop of Canterbury, Randall Davidson, set out the task of the new Board:

> on the one hand to avoid exaggeration as to the powers which can be rightly exercised and the duties which can be rightly discharged by Lay Readers . . . on the other hand, we want to encourage by every means the admirable work which is being done in a perfectly loyal and right way . . .
>
> The Central Board will give coherence, dignity and effectiveness to endeavours which have often suffered for lack of these . . . The Board will recognize the possibilities and the limitations.

Under the Constitution the Archbishops of Canterbury, York and Wales presided, and the Board, which was to meet at least once a year, consisted of two bishops nominated by the Archbishop of Canterbury, and one each from York and Wales. Two representatives (including one lay) were to be elected for each diocese and there were six co-opted places, clerical or lay. An Executive Committee 'with a due proportion of laymen' and representing as far as possible each of the three Provinces was to control the administrative and financial business of the Board.

Its duties included co-ordinating the organization of Readers in the dioceses; maintaining and developing the work of Readers generally, under the authority of the Archbishops and Bishops; and arranging for Annual and other Conferences, and Training Courses. The finances of the Board were to be met by contributions from every DRB, supplementary grants from Societies or the Central Church Fund, and by private donations and subscriptions.

The 1921 Regulations provided the framework for the operation of the Board throughout its life. In 1932, the constitution was revised to allow Church Assembly to appoint six members. Its duties were then extended to include authority to hold examinations for candidates for the office of Reader, to safeguard as far as possible the interests of whole-time stipendiary Readers, and to represent to the Church Assembly such matters as the Board might determine. In 1949, perhaps significantly on the retirement of Dr Claude Blagden, Bishop of Peterborough, who had chaired the Board for 24 years, the Executive Committee was abolished and its powers transferred to the smaller Management Committee.

Much of the main work of the Board was achieved through its sub-committees. While in general the relationship between the committees and the Board remained co-operative, there were times when strains and even power struggles became apparent. In 1968, for example, the Management Committee attempted to influence discussions concerning the integration of CRB with ACCM. The Committee agreed unanimously that 'to facilitate the business of CRB, all commissions and individuals appointed by the Board should send their reports via the Management Committee'. It recognized that it had no power to make changes in such reports *but for the guidance of the Board it might send out accompanying memorandum'* (my italics). Usually such tensions only surfaced when one or two members had held on to their positions for too long, and were unable to move forward in response to changing circumstances and new opportunities.

The work of Central Readers' Board

While all DRBs might be represented on CRB, the Readers in some dioceses were not organized at all, and it was not until 1945 that Bath and Wells became a member. To begin with, some dioceses were very suspicious of CRB. In 1929, after one year as Organizing Secretary, Dr Murray reported that he had visited sixteen dioceses, but some were asking, 'What do we get out of Central Office?' Though he had discovered a dead weight of prejudice against any form of centralization, he was not out to make good people feel uncomfortable. 'London must give practical proof that it is ready to go to Newcastle, if it is to expect the North, from time to time, to come to London.' Many Readers in the Northern Province would still echo that sentiment – leaving Truro Readers feeling even more remote! Murray could only continue his travels to the dioceses, sharing his inspiration at annual conferences, coaxing without compelling.

By the outbreak of war in 1939, when Murray was in his early eighties, he was still looking forward. 'Each Diocesan Board has its own tradition and its own constitution. The Central Board helps them to pool experience and suggest common lines of conduct.' Alongside the work of CRB and its Organizing Secretary, *The Reader* magazine was also working hard to link Readers with one another, to encourage dioceses to look beyond their own boundaries and to share their expertise, and to strengthen the ties between the dioceses and CRB and its office (see Chapter 9).

The next big step forward occurred almost a generation later, when Canon George King took the initiative and arranged a meeting of Wardens and Secretaries in the Northern Provinces in 1960. Twenty-one people attended, and it was acclaimed as 'the most successful meeting CRB had ever organized'. This was the first of what has since become an annual meeting for Wardens, and was followed by annual meetings of diocesan secretaries.

The Board spent most of its time on Reader training, both before and after admission, and on the interpretation of the regulations, especially where dioceses lagged behind, or where Readers were doing more than was permitted in response to pastoral need. In almost every case where the regulations were eventually extended, Readers had already been performing the duties, possibly for a generation or more. Thus CRB was given great scope!

One item on the agenda for some thirty years was the 'uniform' Readers were to wear when performing their duties. As Readers began to be seen more often in church rather than in unconsecrated buildings, and as the robing of choirs became more widespread, and the increasing use of vestments assumed a greater significance in the life of some churches, so Readers seem to have felt a need for some distinctive mark. Most DRBs responded by permitting the wearing of a diocesan badge attached to a ribbon of a regulation colour, width and length. (The variety of such badges may be seen on display in Church House, by courtesy of Church House Corporation to whom they are on permanent loan.)

It seems incredible that so much of the Board's time should have been spent on the topic of uniform, but in 1958 the blue scarf was authorized and within ten years almost all dioceses had adopted it. So the normal wear for Readers is cassock, surplice and blue scarf with the hood of a degree where appropriate. In churches where cassock-albs are customary, the blue scarf may also be worn. The uniform is the same for men and for women.

Towards the end of its life, CRB gave some attention to the timing and style of its meetings. As early as 1925, diocesan representatives pleaded for an increased number of representatives to allow some of the younger DRB members to attend. With a membership of over 100, no action was taken, but the problem of encouraging younger members remains a concern of the present Central Readers' Conference.

The annual meeting was somewhat hesitantly transferred to a *Saturday* in March, but it was not until 1967 that the first residential meeting of the Board was held over a weekend, at Bristol. This has since become the established pattern, with the March meeting in London, and the summer conference hosted on behalf of CRB (now Central Readers' Conference) by Readers in one of the dioceses. In 1972 the Chair, Robert Martineau, Bishop of Blackburn, again suggested opening up the summer meeting, with a brief summer school open to all Readers, followed immediately by the usual Board business meeting.

The opening-up of the CRB meetings was taken a step further the following year. During the 1930s this male body had addressed one another as 'Brother', a form of address accorded in the minutes. By 1973, however, and possibly in anticipation of increasing numbers of women Readers, a suggestion was put forward that Readers' wives (not 'spouses'!) might be invited to attend. Though the Board decided against inviting 'wives, husbands, friends', they were present in 1975, when the conference was held at Kesteven College in Lincoln diocese. The wives had come to stay!

Any national committee, ecclesiastical or otherwise, finds itself occasionally dealing with miscellaneous items which defy categorization. CRB was no exception. From a whole range of possible topics I draw attention to three. In 1931, R. J. Russell MP wrote to the office asking for names of other Reader MPs, so that they might be invited to join with lay ministers of all denominations 'to co-operate in combatting the moral and social evils of the day'. There appears to be no information following up this initiative.

In 1943, Readers in rural areas were in great difficulty because of petrol rationing. CRB took up their case, and they were treated like the clergy and allowed sufficient petrol to discharge their duties as Readers.

At the end of the war, in 1945, Church Assembly published *Towards the Conversion of England*, a Report of a Commission on Evangelism. This report was warmly welcomed at the time, when all were looking forward to new opportunities which peace and restructuring in Church and society would bring. As so often with official Church reports, Readers felt with some justice undervalued, as to both their role within the Church, and their influence in their places of work. There was no mention of Readers in the sections either on 'The Part of the Laity in Evangelism' or 'The Training of the Church in the Faith'. The Board affirmed Readers as trained laymen whose vocation was precisely to do the work of evangelists. The more varied the secular occupations of Readers, the greater the number of points at which the Church had an evangelist. Their points were well made.

One special occasion which demanded CRB's attention from 1963 was the celebration in 1966 of the centenary of the revival of the office of Reader in the Church of England. First HRH Prince Philip, Duke of Edinburgh, graciously accepted an invitation to become the first Patron of CRB. This royal affirmation of lay ministry gave – and still gives – great encouragement as well as pleasure and pride to all Readers, especially as Prince Philip is well known for voicing basic Christian values in places and on occasions where they might otherwise be ignored.

Secondly a Centenary Service was held at St Paul's Cathedral on 11 June 1966, with the Archbishop of Canterbury as preacher. About two thousand Readers gathered from every diocese in England and Wales and from some dioceses overseas, to give thanks for the privilege of serving God in the office of Reader. The Introduction to the service well reflected the prevailing thoughts:

> . . . The normal duty of Readers is to conduct worship and to expound the Faith from a lay point of view and in lay terms . . .
>
> Through such a true lay ministry the Church and its message are brought into the closest possible contact with the world outside the Church. Readers work side by side with people in all walks of life, think in their terms, and speak their language. The Readers at today's service are drawn from almost every rank and class, and from almost every occupation and profession. There is

truly a New Testament quality about their service to the
Church . . .

Those who were present still recall the day and the service for the
inspiration and encouragement it gave them, together with a sense
of recognition at long last of their voluntary, national lay ministry.

Twenty-five years later preparations are being made for the celebration of the 125th anniversary of the revival of Reader ministry.
The movement has outgrown St Paul's Cathedral, and the celebration
is planned to take place at the National Exhibition Centre in Birmingham. *In essence* little has changed in the service offered by these
lay ministers, though they are now much better trained than their
predecessors.

Finance and staffing

One major topic occupied a good deal of CRB's time and attention
– finance. The Board depended on an extension of the Millward
principle, whereby DRBs contributed to central funds, supplemented
from time to time by individual subscriptions, for no specific provision was made for any kind of central financing as Readers were a
voluntary lay ministry. To begin with, in some dioceses DRBs themselves were only just being established, and had not yet affiliated to
CRB. In 1924 and 1925 only sixteen dioceses subscribed to CRB,
and not all of those met the annual target of two shillings per Reader;
eighteen dioceses paid nothing at all. So it is not surprising that Dr
John Murray had to overcome a degree of defensiveness on his
diocesan visits, especially when he hoped that even the most supportive dioceses would double or even treble their contributions: 'The
Board cannot be judged by what it has done with a wholly inadequate
staff'.

In 1931, the proposal that CRB should become organically linked
with the Church Assembly raised the hopes of some of its members.
The constitution was revised to allow six members appointed by
Church Assembly to sit on CRB. With an annual budget of £400,
the prospect of a grant of £500 from the Central Church Fund was
welcomed, though Murray was quick to see – and to say – that it
was insufficient to allow for future developments.

By 1954 there was little improvement in the overall position. Rents
and salaries accounted for £900, but the Church Assembly grant had
been cut to £300 per annum, and the income from dioceses was by
no means reaching its target level of three shillings per head. Some
Boards generously paid more, but others defaulted. Most DRBs had
given an additional grant to CRB to raise over £400 to re-equip the

office with new furniture and such necessary items as a second-hand addressing machine, a duplicator and two typewriters.

In 1970 the Board was again caught in a vicious circle, with a substantial deficit and consequent staffing difficulties, which meant that subscriptions for the magazine had not been paid, accounts had not been sent out, training was not self-financing. In 1972 the Board decided to double the target figure to £1 per head, and this considerably improved the situation. By 1974 there was a surplus of some £700, but then inflation began to bite and by the following year the surplus was reduced to just over £100.

While CRB was struggling to pay its way, Church Assembly was very anxious to integrate Readers with the Church's ministry. In 1957 it reported that there were many general questions of Reader policy to be considered in relation to the Church's ministry as a whole, but that a voluntary organization should not be financed from central funds. Its grant of £500 per annum remained unchanged for 21 years, despite inflation and other increasing costs. While the financial argument used by the Church Assembly was doubtless legal, and according to some people justifiable, it failed utterly to express any kind of vision for an authorized and episcopally licensed lay ministry, and it evaded its responsibility for the existing organization or future development. It seemed that Readers were being kept in their place in the central life of the Church, while many parishes were increasingly dependent on them on Sundays.

The whole Reader operation was performed on a shoestring. Without the organizing and administrative skills, and the wholehearted dedication, of its two longest-serving honorary secretaries, Dr John Murray (1928–44) and Canon George King, OBE (1956–80), it is doubtful whether Readers could have maintained a national, well-trained, lay ministry movement.

One other person deserves mention. Miss Myland held the operation together in the office from 1937 to her retirement in 1968 as the only full-time paid (perhaps underpaid is a fairer description though not one she would ever have approved) member of staff. She was assisted by a succession of half-time assistants, most of whom are reported to have worked with a sense of dedication and utmost zeal. The Reader movement owes much to their self-sacrificing devotion. When Miss Myland retired a presentation was made to her in appreciation of the great contribution she had made to the work of Readers, and 'on the strict understanding that should she wish to give any or all of the sum to Reader work she should not be regarded as defeating the wishes of the Board'. Characteristic to the last, she most generously donated the money to further the work of Readers.

Thus the Miss Myland Fund was established for the benefit of Readers and their office.

A new era was, however, being inaugurated for the Reader movement as negotiations had already started for the integration of CRB with the Advisory Council for the Church's Ministry.

8: A National Movement 2:
Central Readers' Conference

Part of the whole ministry of the Church

In 1966 the Archbishops of Canterbury and York, on behalf of the Standing Committee of Church Assembly, invited the Central Readers' Board to look at its constitution, pointing out that it now had 108 members. This apparently reasonable request sent CRB sailing through squally seas for the next decade!

There were two fundamental reasons for the Archbishops' concern. First, the source of authority regulating the office of Reader had changed, from the Archbishops and Bishops in 1905, to the Archbishops acting alone in 1921, to Convocation in 1941, and in the early 1960s to draft Canons which were still awaiting Royal Assent. Second, the Committee on Central Funds saw the need for one body concerned with the best use of all of the Church's human resources.

During 1966 the newly named and constituted Advisory Council for the Church's Ministry was directed 'to promote the most effective ministry, both of men and women, in the service of the Church and to make appropriate recommendations for this purpose to the Bishops and to the Church Assembly'. It was further directed to keep under review different forms of ministry, ordained and lay; to promote discussion in the Church about adapting its ministry to meet changing pastoral situations; and to keep in close touch with central Church bodies concerned with different forms of ministry, including Readers.

CRB was fortunate in that Sir John Guillum Scott, Secretary of Church Assembly, agreed to give advice and guidance in the negotiations which followed. All who were involved commented on his clarity of mind, his kindness and his unfailing courtesy. It is evident from the records that he was a man of great wisdom, tact and infinite patience and good humour. He drew up a draft constitution proposing a Board of 25 members, not necessarily members of Church Assembly but appointed by its Standing Committee, to hold office for five years coterminous with the House of Laity of Church Assembly.

The proposed Board's functions included working with ACCM to promote the most effective use of Readers in the service of the Church; advising the Bishops, Convocations and Church Assembly in all matters relating to Readers; co-ordinating the work of DRBs; arranging an Annual General Meeting with two representatives from each DRB; and generally promoting the work of Readers. CRB was already performing some of these tasks. In the accompanying memorandum Scott made it very clear that the primary function of the Board was 'to be a thinking, policy-making and directing body'.

It is evident from a statement from CRB's then Chairman, the Rt Rev. George Reindorp, Bishop of Guildford, that such major proposals for change came at a bad time for CRB. Its Management Committee was already divided by tensions between members, most of whom were elderly, with between ten and 24 years' continuous service. It was apparent to Bishop Reindorp that many younger Readers would have welcomed changes. 'What we really need', one had written, 'is a good radical working party to rethink what we ought to be up to . . . At present we are something of a fuddy-duddy lot, but we could be so different.'

Negotiations dragged on throughout 1967, but the negotiating committee elected by CRB was itself divided, and advised the Board not to rush precipitately into a decision. One member, Mr T. M. Phillips of Bristol, issued a supplementary statement:

> Few Readers look to the CRB as a Trade Union but as the co-ordinating body which will relate the Office of Reader to the total life of the Church, and this can only be done by an integral unit evolving in the swiftly changing pattern of Church government. We are already late in the day for our voice to be heard on several matters closely concerning our office.

The debates were totally unrealistic. It was said that there was no need for ACCM to take over and absorb CRB; consultation between Church Assembly and CRB should be on equal terms: CRB should not be subservient to Church Assembly. There was 'wild talk' about CRB being misled, and breaches of faith. No wonder Scott commented that the present Readers' Board was not very highly thought of by the younger Readers in the House of Laity, and wrote jokingly of the war hotting up and needing his bullet-proof vest when he next met the Board!

Yet there were those who saw that the proposals would bring CRB into the mainstream of thinking about changing roles of ministry, and provide essential channels of communication with ACCM and Church Assembly. Bishop Reindorp made the position very clear in a letter to Board members: 'The responsibility for determining the conditions of service and standards of Readers rests with the whole Church and not with Readers themselves . . . In fact the responsibility will rest with General Synod.' Common sense finally prevailed at the Annual General Meeting in March 1968, when the Board approved a constitution under which it agreed to become a Board of Church Assembly.

Having delayed so long in making a decision, no action could be taken immediately, owing to the impending publication of the report of the Committee on the Boards and Councils of General Synod (Church Assembly no. 1173). This Committee proposed a Board of Ministry responsible for the selection, training, and examination of all ministers, ordained and lay, including Readers. The programme for restructuring all work was planned over a five-year period, with the transfer of the existing responsibilities of CRB in the third phase, when the future of the Board itself would have to be considered.

Again the response was defensive. ACCM would not be able to give sufficient time or attention to lay ministries; it would show bias to the ordained ministry; the expertise and experience of CRB would be ignored; even 'we suffer everywhere from prejudice to Readers and much ill-informed criticism'. In July 1970 the Chairman reported that Church Assembly, not surprisingly as it was about to be superseded by General Synod, had taken no action on the report, and that CRB would probably have to continue operating in its present form, raising its own funds, apart from a continuation of the Central Board of Finance grant of £500, for the next three years.

There the matter rested until 1975 when an agreed basis for discussion was worked out by the Honorary Secretary, Mr Derek Pattinson, Secretary General of General Synod, and Canon Hugh Melinsky, Chief Secretary of ACCM. A small Joint Working Party recommended in January 1976 that a Readers' Committee be established under the chairmanship of a diocesan bishop (later amended to a member of the House of Bishops) who should be a member of ACCM; that CRB be reconstituted and renamed Central Readers' Conference; that consideration be given to the appointment ultimately of two full-time staff to deal with the work of the Readers' Committee; that the present staff be seconded to ACCM, with office accommodation adjacent to ACCM offices; and that diocesan contributions for Readers be administered by the Central Board of Finance. The report was presented to the Annual General Meeting with an encouraging note from Dr John Botterill, Vice-Chairman of CRB, and a member of the working party.

Synod has not paid adequate attention to the potential of Reader

ministry because there has been no one to speak for it in
ACCM . . . We would have our contribution to make and would
also be able to gain for ourselves if we came within an enlarged
ACCM . . . It is not a scheme whereby the Central Board of
Finance takes over our assets. Rather, the Central Board of Finance generously offers us their experience and service . . . but it
will remain for us . . . to develop our own financial policy to
support our different activities.

After discussion, the Board approved the recommendations without
opposition. New constitutions were worked out, both for the Readers'
Committee and for CRC, in consultation with senior members of
General Synod staff and the Charity Commissioners. Though by
the constitution the Readers' Committee was technically an ACCM
Committee, CRB was happy to accept the new arrangement, which
came into effect on 1 January 1977.

Why did the integration of the organization of Readers with ACCM
take ten years to accomplish? When one recalls the very gradual
development of Reader ministry during the first hundred years, and
the extreme caution of many clergy and laity towards a lay ministry
which the needs of the Church, both liturgically and pastorally, called
forth, it is not difficult to understand why some Readers became
defensive. By 1966 CRB had become unrepresentative of Readers as
a whole. Its members, though proud of CRB's independence, and of
its good record of being financially self-supporting through diocesan
contributions, failed to grasp the significance of the opportunity to
become, and to be seen to be, part of the whole ministry of the
Church as expressed through its organization. In the five years
between 1970 and 1975 there were changes in the membership of
CRB. Ideas which had once seemed strange and too challenging
became more familiar and acceptable. When CRB agreed to become
integrated with ACCM it took a big step forward, one which the
majority of Readers have never regretted.

In partnership with ACCM

In 1982 a working group was set up to review the first five years. It
recommended that

CRC should authorize its Executive Committee to enter into a
wide discussion within ACCM on this developing incorporation
of Readers' work within its structure; regarding only as essential
that the Chairman of CRC remains a full member of ACCM and
thereby one of ACCM bishops.

The report of this joint ACCM–CRC working group, *Readers in ACCM: The Next Phase*, led to further changes. The functions of the Readers' Committee were divided, so that those which pertained to CRC became the responsibility of its newly-named Executive Committee, and those pertaining to ACCM were transferred to a restructured Lay Ministry Committee. This committee became responsible for advising General Synod through ACCM on the five Lay Ministries governed by Canon, namely Deaconesses (now very few in number as most have become deacons and no new candidates for deaconess are accepted), Accredited Lay Workers, Readers, Church Army Evangelists and Religious.

CRC, through its Executive, retained responsibility for *communications* through Conference meetings, *The Reader*, and its relationships with Wardens and diocesan secretaries; *courses*, including Selwyn and the Readers' and Preachers' Conference; and *community* within the movement though its own life and work, its contact with Reader members of General Synod, and its availability to Readers seeking information, encouragement and guidance.

CRC's relationship with ACCM was mainly expressed in three ways: *representational*, whereby CRC is invited to submit nominations to ACCM for membership of ACCM Committees involved in Readers' work; *organizational*, whereby the Honorary Secretary liaises with the Secretary of the Lay Ministry Committee and its work, attends ACCM Executive staff meetings when Readers' matters are discussed and presents an annual report; and *advisory*, whereby CRC though its officials and representatives is able to advise ACCM at appropriate levels on all matters relating to Reader ministry. Additionally, in 1986, responsibility for Reader training was transferred to ACCM's Committee for Theological Education, with CRC acting as its agent.

Three recent working party reports on Selection, Training, and Bishops' Regulations (see Chapter 15) provide a good example of the working out of the partnership between CRC and ACCM. Communication is two-way: the Readers have the opportunity to draw on the expertise of ACCM staff and the wider circle of the members of ACCM committees. At the same time they also have an opportunity through their representatives of feeding information into ACCM committees, particularly from the Reader and lay ministry point of view. My experience on the Committee for Ministerial Education is that Readers are given a sympathetic hearing, and that there are some occasions when a lay view adds another dimension to the discussion.

The increasing confidence of both partners owes much to two people: the recently retired Chief Secretary of ACCM, Canon Timothy Tyndall, for his encouragement of Readers and Reader ministry and for his wise, unruffled leadership; and Mr C. J. Ball, who during his term as Honorary Secretary of CRC furthered Readers' interests in ACCM circles with commendable propriety. With the restructuring of ACCM into an Advisory Board of Ministry further changes lie ahead, but Readers are not likely to find them as daunting in the future as they were in the past.

Readers' leaders

Throughout their history both CRB and CRC have been fortunate in their Chairmen. The Rt Rev. Claude Blagden, Bishop of Peterborough and Chairman from 1928 to 1949, was instrumental in consolidating the work of CRB and speaking on behalf of Readers in Church Assembly when their very legality was being questioned. The Rt Rev. George Reindorp, Bishop of Guildford, was Chairman from 1961 to 1971. His wise guidance and forbearance ultimately prevailed during a period which reflected both the achievement of Readers in the centenary celebrations, and their lack of trust in the crucial negotiations with Church Assembly and ACCM. The Rt Rev. Robert Martineau, Bishop of Huntingdon and then of Blackburn, was himself a Reader before ordination. His book, *The Office and Work of a Reader* (Mowbray, 1970) had incalculable influence on the training, life and work of Readers for a generation.

More recently the Rt Rev. John Waine, now Bishop of Chelmsford, steered CRC as it worked out its closer relationship with the ACCM. When I attended my first Readers' conference in 1981, as one of only three women representatives, my first impression was of an old boys' reunion of very old boys. John Waine gently encouraged, and patiently and with good humour nudged members forward into the future, thus preparing the way for his successor, the Rt Rev. Michael Baughen, Bishop of Chester, to continue the work with his customary verve as Readers prepare to celebrate the 125th anniversary of the revival of their office.

The most outstanding contribution to the national Reader movement was undoubtedly made by Dr John Murray, who worked with Readers for over sixty years. 'There is no department of Readers' life and work which has not been enriched by his example and strengthened by his teaching', wrote Charles F. Shepherd in a memoir (published CRB, 1973). As early as 1923 the *Church Family Newspaper* described Murray as 'the heart and brains of the whole movement . . . the inspiring force'.

As Principal of the Summer Courses or 'Selwyn', he was well known for his intellectual stimulus, spiritual guidance, and the ways in which he could put people at their ease, draw out different points of view and open up vistas of truth. Underneath was a strong motivating force for what he called, and sometimes lectured on, *the Prophethood of the Laity*. His work at Selwyn built up Readers individually and corporately. As one 'fellow worker' wrote at his death, 'Who can assess the number of those who have survived this greatly gifted and wise teacher . . . scattered over the country and the world? . . . They will thank God for Murray's attractive personality, high ideals and transparent goodness.'

His work for Readers in general, as Chair of the Annual Conference on Readers' work, then as Honorary Treasurer of CRB, and later, on his retirement as Master of Selwyn College, as Honorary Organizing Secretary from 1928 to 1944, not only built up the Reader movement nationally, but assured its place within the life of the Church of England. 'His clear vision, firm conviction, calm courage, constant persistence, hard work and patient prayers' laid firm foundations for the future growth of the Reader movement while many of his contemporaries were querying its very survival.

The Rev. George King attended his first CRB meeting in 1948, and became a member of the Management Committee a few years later. Already Honorary Secretary and Examiner for Winchester Diocesan Readers' Board since 1947, in 1956 his appointment as Honorary Secretary of CRB was welcomed with acclaim, and he served with distinction for 25 years.

Rector of the small parishes of Stoke Charity with Hunton, Canon King (he became an Honorary Canon of Winchester Cathedral in 1958) combined his interest in Readers with the Chair of Hampshire County Youth Committee, to which he gave some twenty years' service and for which he was awarded the OBE. As Honorary Secretary of CRB he carried a heavy burden during the negotiations with Church Assembly and ACCM, and in setting CRC on its way. Two important events occurred during this period. The first was the centenary celebrations, and the second the admission of women in 1969.

Throughout his period in office he took a very active interest in raising the standard of Reader training, both before and after admission. Like Dr Murray, he too worked hard to maintain the high standard of Selwyn Summer Courses, both academically, and spiritually as their chaplain for many years. He continued as Chairman of the Selwyn Committee to celebrate the centennial year in 1981. He also continued the Murray tradition of visiting diocesan conferences and establishing links with DRBs.

One of Canon King's most important achievements was the writing of *Readers: A Pioneer Ministry* (published by the Miss Myland Fund, 1973, to which he generously gave all the profits). It is a scholarly and factual account of Reader ministry from the early Church to 1972, to which all Readers, the present writer included, must be indebted. The author is objective and self-effacing, yet the title reveals King's feeling for the Reader ministry, together with his realization of its importance both to and for the Church. The whole Reader movement was delighted when the Archbishop of Canterbury conferred a Lambeth Doctor of Divinity degree upon him. I suspect he 'retired' as reluctantly as many Readers do, when asked to exchange their licences for permission to officiate. Now in his eighties he still maintains a lively interest in everything to do with Readers.

Canon King was followed by Mr C. J. Ball, a Reader from Rochester diocese, who held office from 1981 to 1988 as Honorary Secretary of CRC, and also of ACCM's Readers' Committee during its lifetime from 1981 to 1986. What was described as a part-time appointment for two to three days a week became for Jim, as he is known to his contemporaries, almost a full-time occupation with many weekends spent visiting annual Readers' conferences in the dioceses. His understanding of the Reader movement, coupled with his meticulous attention to detail, and his personal commitment (and that of his wife Mary) to the work, facilitated many developments. As a Reader himself, Jim was able in his quiet way to extend an understanding of, and respect for, Readers among ACCM's staff and committees. He never missed an opportunity either to speak on behalf of Readers in the Church at large, or to encourage individual Readers or diocesan officers who came to him for advice.

To Brian Field, the present Honorary Secretary, belongs the task of continuing and developing work already begun, and organizing, with the help of a committee, the celebrations for the 125th anniversary of the revival of the office of Reader.

Achievements and prospects

When CRB first met in 1922, Readers did not quite fit into the Church Assembly's organization, yet they could not be ignored (especially with the weight of the Master of Selwyn, the Archbishops and certain bishops behind them). Readers have gradually been integrated into the life, work and ministry of the whole Church. They now have office accommodation and facilities in Church House as part of ACCM, and part-time secretarial staff paid from ACCM's budget, both for CRC matters and for training. Alongside this much appreciated and much needed financial support, CRC has sufficient resources from the dioceses to continue to develop its work in partnership with them. The Chairman of CRC is a member of ACCM (and its successor the Advisory Board of Ministry), and one of the ACCM bishops. There are Reader representatives on appropriate ACCM committees. In these and other ways Readers are gradually taking their place as lay ministers within the organization of the Church.

Progress at the centre is being matched in dioceses where some DRBs are also being integrated into Boards or Councils of Ministry, but such progress is by no means uniform. As numbers increase to over 8,000 Readers with another 1,600 in training (December 1989 figures), and as the numbers of Readers licensed each year exceeds the numbers of those ordained, the work both in dioceses and at the centre is unlikely to lessen.

The question of staffing must now be faced much more realistically. This does not, of course, imply any criticism of present or former staff, who are all noted in their different ways for dedicated and unstinting service, nor of the members of the Executive Committee for the responsibilities they share among them. Some seventy years ago, long before he became Honorary Organizing Secretary, Dr Murray was arguing the necessity for a full-time Organizing Secretary, supported by appropriate secretarial staff and office facilities. Although almost all dioceses are pleased to subscribe a capitation fee to maintain the work of CRC, there is no reason why Readers should have to continue to rely on these 'voluntary' contributions to provide for the expenses of its honorary staff members.

As Readers are now recognized as an integral part of the ministry of the whole Church, is it not time that the movement should be serviced by a full-time Reader, man or woman, paid from central Church funds, in the same way that lay people are employed by General Synod's other departments, for example the Board of Education? Voluntary workers would still have a contribution to make, but the Church through its representatives in General Synod might rest assured that that part of its ministry which is exercised by its trained and licensed Readers was no longer trading on the devotion and self-sacrifice of willing individuals and their families. Perhaps an added bonus for both Church and Readers might be that it would be feasible to appoint a younger Reader to the helm!

The development of a national Reader movement has not been one of smooth sailing all the way. While the ship itself has proved seaworthy, there have been stormy episodes, times when issues have been beclouded by fog, and times when a change of course was unwelcome to at least some of the crew. Despite all this, Readers have been fortunate in their leaders at the centre. If Readers are to survive, they need continuing effective leadership by their Honorary Officers, staff and committee members. But CRC (soon perhaps to be renamed Central Readers' Council), must build on the achievements of the past and work in partnership with both ACCM and the dioceses. The continuing working out of this partnership may well, from time to time, necessitate living with tension and sometimes taking risks. Readers need one another: they also need, though they may not always welcome, that part of the Church which is expressed through its ecclesiastical institutions. More important still, Readers need a corporate awareness of the God who calls to a lay ministry which serves not just the Church but the whole community.

9: Bringing people together: *The Reader*

> To bring people together, to break down isolation, to build on what is being achieved at Keble and Selwyn, to open up subjects of practical and pressing interest, to learn about diocesan organization for lay work . . .

These were the objects of *The Reader and Lay Worker* which Dr John Murray set out in his 'Godspeed' message in the first issue in January 1904. He himself had already had some practical experience in the field as the editor of its predecessor, *Readers' Work: Notes and News for Licensed Readers*, published from 1896 by the London Diocesan Readers' Board, but circulated much more widely. The first editors, two clergy and two Readers, envisaged *The Reader and Lay Worker* as helping those engaged in church work, reflecting the whole range of ecclesiastical outlook, and setting down 'plainly and authoritatively' what was permitted and what was not, at home and abroad.

The immediate reaction to the first issue of *The Reader and Lay Worker* was generally encouraging, though some thought it dull, and others complained of too many advertisements. In reply to the latter the editors were quick to point out that a subvention of £100 would be sufficient to eliminate them. Incidentally, after many years of cover advertisements only, the advertisements are back again – for the same purpose!

The Reader and Lay Worker, later to become *The Lay Reader*, and subsequently *The Reader*, has been an integral part of the Reader movement for most of its active life, especially if one assumes that only with the publication of the 1905 Regulations had the movement really 'arrived'. Ask Readers today what they remember about *The Reader* and most, I suspect, would look a little nonplussed. Yet most would agree with the person who, when asked how many sermons she could remember, replied, 'Sermons are like food: I can't remember the menus but I know I've been well fed'. The main diet of *The Reader* has always provided a number of staple items: information and reflections on Reader ministry; main articles of a spiritual, biblical or theological nature; practical advice on various aspects of a Reader's work; training pages; news and notes; discussion and correspondence; the gazette of Readers admitted and licensed; overseas news (especially in earlier volumes); and for many years the minutes of its central organization. The Readers have been well fed!

Serving the individual

The individual is given personal significance from the moment he or she is admitted and licensed to Readership, for the diocesan list, provided it is submitted, is printed in the gazette. Names are repeated when people are relicensed in other parishes or dioceses. Subscription lists, acknowledging contributions of one shilling (five pence in present terms) and more, were featured in earlier volumes of the *Lay Reader*, particularly for the Lay Reader Studentship Association (see Chapter 13) and for the Headquarters Fund.

Some people find their names in print through a mention in Notes or Personal News, and their friends may celebrate their lives in personal tributes in the obituary notices. Nowadays such notices tend to be brief, but formerly they were more expansive in content and style. In March 1914, for example, Geoffrey Bickwell of Exeter Diocese is remembered as one

> who for more than a quarter of a century has gone in and out of our vicarages and schools with an ever-growing welcome and affection alike from children and teachers and clergy . . . Our diocese is indeed the richer for his bright example. God has not seen fit to give him any rest or retirement here, but we can well be sure he has gone hence to higher and happier service.

Contrast this obituary with that in 1924 of Llewellyn A. Cynfaen Evans, founder and first secretary of St Asaph Diocesan Lay Readers Union. A fluent preacher in Welsh and English and an authority on Welsh literature, he became 'from conscientious motives' a stipendiary Reader. 'His whole heart was in his work and he won golden opinions in every parish in which he ministered . . . At no time did he receive a wage equal to that of a roadsweeper.' Always he had to move on because a priest was appointed in his place. On one occasion he had accepted a new post, packed all his goods ready for removal, only to be told that the engagement was cancelled as the bishop would not license a Reader. So he was left stranded and unemployed for six months. Finally he obtained another appointment. On the first Sunday, after a six-mile walk to the station, he took the Sunday morning service but was taken ill and died at the roadside on the way to a Mission church. As a result of this obituary notice over £100 was subscribed by Readers from his own diocese and all over the country for his invalid wife and daughter.

Promoting Reader ministry and training

Ten years before Llewellyn Evans died, The *Lay Reader* had published an outspoken article entitled 'The Oppression of the Hireling'. It described the case of a Reader who was given notice to leave 'without a word of blame or hint of inefficiency'. His advertisement for a new post, inserted under an assumed name and with a distant address, resulted in an answer from his own vicar! 'The truth is that until the clergy learn to apply ordinary commercial morality, to say nothing of Christian principles, to their conditions of employment it is quite hopeless to attempt to improve the lot of the paid Reader.' Fortunately such a strongly worded article on behalf of Readers is no longer needed today, though there are still laypeople – and a few clergy too – whose experiences of the Church as employer are equally underserved and almost as unhappy. Such cases are seldom reported in the Church press, let alone becoming the subject of comment, as 'discretion' rules!

The Reader was the principal means of keeping Readers in touch with all kinds of events. Information about Selwyn courses, and latterly the Joint Readers' and Preachers' Conferences, and other training events, are included in the 'Notes' or 'Notices'. In 1914 Mowbray's Almanacs and Kalendars were recommended, priced from one penny upwards. There are items on Reader ministry itself in almost every issue, sometimes in the form of addresses at services of admission, or articles relating to the recognition of Reader ministry, as in 1934 when the Banns of Marriage Measure was being debated. Two snippets give the flavour. The first is from the Bishop of Colchester's address to newly admitted Readers in 1934:

> Don't forget the inner shrine by your prayers and meditations, in your Bible and Communion. You go from Christ . . . Go with all the glow and enthusiasm of those who have been with Christ, and men will 'take knowledge of you, that you have been with Jesus'.

The second is entitled 'The Case for the Official Recognition of the Office of Reader by Convocation' and is the end of a letter which was circulated to all members of the Convocations of Canterbury and York, signed by John Millward, Julian Smith, and W. S. Williams among others:

It seems to us that certain Churchmen generally will not believe in the commission of a Reader until there is canonical recognition of the office or until they see an Admission Service in the Prayer Book. Such a service should contain such directions as will leave no doubt as to the part the Reader is authorized to take in the public services of the Church.

If the Church needs and welcomes their services, as Bishops and clergy have repeatedly stated, Readers will continue to spend themselves in the service of the Church; but the Church should show this definitely.

It is significant that senior members and officers of CRB felt compelled to write in this way. The printing of the letter in *The Reader* must have heartened many Readers throughout the dioceses.

The Reader has always played a major part in Reader training by providing information and articles directly linked with pre-admission examinations and post-admission continuation courses. Publicity through *The Reader* was instrumental in 1934 in changing the date of the examination from mid-September to the more convenient mid-October. Interestingly, the notice of the examinations was printed every month from April to October. Did the Readers in training not see the magazine regularly, or were their tutors remiss in noting the relevant information? In November and December the examination questions for each of the four papers were published. The 'Notes' report that the examiners had been 'successful in propounding questions that demanded thought rather than the mere exercise of memory'. There were fifty entrants from eleven dioceses, with arrangements 'cheerfully made . . . at seventeen centres at which friendly clergymen were invigilating'. What more was needed to encourage the uncertain to 'have a go'?

Articles, reviews and correspondence

Going through the volumes of *The Reader* at ten-yearly intervals one finds similar themes, but expressed in the language of the day. Few people today would think of describing Oral Prayer, which 'begins where meditation ends', under the headings of Supplication, Deprecation, Obsecration, Intercession and Ejaculation. Biblical articles abound: Dr Murray's monthly study notes and scholarly expositions infused with a warm humanity; studies of Amos, Hosea and Isaiah, the set books for examination; five articles on 'Israel's Wisdom Literature'; 'John's Apocalyptic Teaching'; twelve articles on specific Old Testament passages. A series of six articles on 'The Problem of Wealth' in 1914 differs from our expectations today. A quick introduction was followed by 'The Deuteronomic Code', 'The Greeks and the Preparation for Christianity' (two articles), and 'The Latter Days', before reaching 'The Problem Today'.

Other series included 'Christian Belief' and 'Some Elements of the Philosophy of Religion'. There were a few Church history topics, and others on spiritual healing; medical missions and new developments in mission; magic and witchcraft; and the Boy Scout movement. In 1974, when Series 3 Morning Prayer and Evening Prayer were published, there was an article entitled '1662 – A Treasury of Praise and Prayer'. Articles in 1944 looked towards reconstruction at the end of the war, but by 1954 the articles were inward-looking. In 1989 articles included 'The Reader as Preacher', 'Do You Believe and Trust in the Holy Spirit?', 'Faith and Secular Employment', 'The Education Act 1988', and 'Ethical Investments'.

The first volume of the *Lay Reader and Church Worker* included practical advice on all kinds of parochial activities (see Chapter 2). This aspect continued in later volumes, though with some modification. In 1914 'Work among Men and Lads' was followed by an 'Outline Address to Men' with twelve literary quotations. Sermon notes were included in all the early volumes, and were demanded again when they were dropped. As time passed there was more emphasis on the ministry of preaching, with six articles on the 'Art and Craft of Preaching' in 1954, and ten years later a further series, this time by the Director of the College of Preachers.

Encouragement to continue reading has always been an important feature of *The Reader*. Six articles entitled 'The Christian's Bookshelf' were written by Readers in 1944; 'Required Reading' 1974 explained how to study for the Archbishops' Diploma, allowing five years part-time. Book reviews appear in every issue. Twenty-seven books were reviewed in 1944, and 112 in 1964, the year following the publication of *Honest to God*. Of these, 22 were biblical commentaries or interpretations. Other titles reviewed included *The Abolition of Religion, Faith and the Space Age*, and *Faith and Modern Error*, alongside *Christian Belief, Christian Faith, Christian Maturity, Christian Mysteries*, and *Christian Priesthood*. Three books were significant for very different reasons: Ian Ramsey's *Religion and Science: Conflict and Synthesis*; Leslie Paul's *The Deployment and Payment of the Clergy*; and, edited by Stephen Neill and Hans Ruedi Weber, *The Layman in Christian History*.

Readers have never been able to complain that they did not know what was available, even though access to books might have presented problems. Most clergy have been, and still are, generous in lending their books to Readers, especially to those in training. Sometimes Readers lend *their* books to encourage the clergy to read!

The correspondence columns of the Church press generally offer readers an opportunity to express their deep concerns and prejudices. Whether it is because the editors of *The Reader* have used their skills, or Readers save their purple passages for their preaching, I am not sure, but apart from pleas on behalf of stipendiary Readers the language of the letters is surprisingly restrained. Few letters break new ground.

In 1974 there were criticisms of the new Archbishops' Diploma for Readers: 'Just what are the features which make it "more attractive"? The reading list is at least ten times as long as that for any university degree . . . and what has the Reader then achieved?' and another: 'To my mind the books are not relevant enough . . . Readers are a bridge between pulpit and pew . . . I wish the Archbishops' Diploma for Readers could be made more realistic and relevant.' Needless to say, the arguments of both correspondents were rebutted by those who had already been awarded the Diploma.

Some letters are challenging: do we read too much – ephemeral newspapers and journals – and too little 'solid, permanent and inspiring literature'? This called for several replies, one regretting his own incumbent's 'coarse, vulgar and wordly' Sunday newspapers (perhaps the cleric was only trying to find out what his congregation were reading!). Why are clergy always included in intercessions and Readers apparently never? Do Readers need the prayers of the congregation or are they past praying for? When are sermons 'sermons', and when are they 'snacks'? What do we mean by 'inspiration of the Scriptures', and should we not take fundamentalism seriously?

Linking the dioceses and Central Readers' Board
In the first volume of *The Reader and Lay Worker* (1904) there were accounts of diocesan activities in London, Ripon, Llandaff, Durham and Worcester. This cross-fertilization of ideas and practice between the dioceses has always been a feature of *The Reader* and another key to its continuity. *The Reader* is circulated to all diocesan bishops and Wardens so that they may be aware of current thinking among Readers. Those who write articles on the Reader movement in their dioceses find that the exercise demands a time of stocktaking and reflection. Many of the articles have sparked off ideas in other dioceses and led to the spread of better practice in diocesan administration. Sometimes the differences between large, mainly rural dioceses such as Carlisle, Lincoln or Exeter, and small, compact, mainly urban dioceses like Manchester or Birmingham, give rise to different

problems and different solutions in matters of training and encouraging Christian fellowship.

Diocesan articles made it possible, especially in the early days, for overseas dioceses to share their particular concerns and to feel part of a larger communion. More recently there has been a growing appreciation of partnership between dioceses at home and overseas, exemplified in Christina Baxter's article 'Partners in Mission' in 1989.

From 1922 to 1965 the minutes of the Proceedings of Central Readers' Board were published in full in *The Reader*, so that all Readers, and especially DRB officers, were kept in close touch with the centre. This was extremely important at a time when DRBs themselves were in process of formation and consolidation. Just as the dioceses had to rely on parishes with Readers for financial support, so CRB had to rely on contributions from DRBs, and even from individual Readers, to make ends meet. Some DRBs consistently failed in their support, through poverty, negligence or lack of organization, but others were very generous. This explains why the subscriptions and offerings received by CRB were published in full; and why, as late as 1950, when the office needed to buy furniture and basic office equipment, a special appeal was made to the dioceses for the necessary funds. Only two refused.

Each Diocesan Readers' Board had its own traditions and constitution. *The Reader* helped them to pool their experience. With the publication of CRB minutes all Readers could become aware of what was going on nationally, and could relate it to their own ministry. In 1954, for example, a letter from a Reader in Southwell diocese began 'It must be very disconcerting to some Readers to realize that CRB should find it necessary to appeal to, almost implore, Diocesan Boards to pay their annual subscriptions . . .'. His plea for a greater sense of financial responsibility among DRBs and their individual Readers must have cheered CRB members.

It is significant that CRB's minutes ceased to be published in the centenary year, when negotiations with Church Assembly and ACCM were beginning. Since then there has been no *direct* communication between the Board, now Central Readers' Conference, and Readers, though of course its thinking and decision making has been published through news or notes or articles as appropriate.

Despite the varying fortunes of *The Reader*, Readers themselves have little excuse for being ill-informed about their immediate concerns. Increasingly they have themselves contributed articles and reviews. This is not to say that there is universal satisfaction with *The Reader*, but at least those who are most critical have an opportunity to improve it.

Growth and development

Turning from content to the production of the magazine, there have been two changes of title. Just two years after its launching as *The Reader and Lay Worker*, its title was changed to *The Lay Reader* because the publishers of *The Daily Chronicle* launched a new magazine called *The Reader* with anticipated sales of over 200,000. The title *The Lay Reader* remained until January 1948 when it became *The Reader*, to coincide with the official designation of the office of Reader in the Church of England.

Between 1939 and 1949 costs doubled and postage trebled, yet the price had remained unchanged for almost its lifetime! Rising costs led to the adoption of a smaller format in 1948, and to a bi-monthly issue in 1971. Between October 1973 and July 1974 costs rose again by almost a third, necessitating a change to a quarterly publication, though with the same number of pages as in the bi-monthly edition. A quarterly edition is still maintained, with 160 pages including advertising.

This bare outline of the development of *The Reader* hides much anxiety concerning its viability. In early days of crisis it survived only through the generosity of individuals and their dioceses. Yet as the number of Readers grew, so the circulation increased; in 1951 4,000 copies were printed for the first time, and by 1990 this figure had doubled. Throughout the life of *The Reader* and its predecessors many copies have been sent to dioceses and individuals overseas.

The life and quality of any periodical owes much to its successive editors, and *The Reader* is no exception. From its inception with two clerical and two Reader editors, A. W. Nott gradually took much of the responsibility, as well as the initiative, to establish the first CRB headquarters in Dean's Yard, which also served as the office for the magazine. Behind the scenes the wisdom and encouragement of Dr Murray were always available until his death in 1944.

After World War II Allan Maynard became editor for a quarter of a century. While there is no denying the hard work that he put in, there were times when his lack of courtesy and judgement led to strained relationships with his colleagues in CRB, and later Central Readers' Conference. A typical example may be found in his handling of the centenary celebrations. The announcement that HRH Prince Philip had agreed to become Patron was apparently inserted against his will and occupied just three or four lines. Nothing further was added in subsequent issues, and there were no signs of the great pleasure with which this event was greeted by Readers all over the country and beyond. Furthermore, without any consultation with the committee or CRB, and without any costing, he produced a Centenary Supplement of 24 pages. Not even the Chairman had an opportunity to contribute to it. Throughout Maynard's last few years as editor, which coincided with the reorganization of the Board into the Central Readers' Conference, relations remained uneasy and some disappointment with *The Reader* was expressed on various occasions.

In 1973 Martin Daly, a very much younger Reader, succeeded him and promised a magazine which was more useful and solid, less gossipy and parochial. Daly's period as editor was dogged by inflation and difficulties of production which took some time to overcome. An article entitled 'Universalism, the Forgotten Tradition?', published in November 1979, caused a strong reaction and gave him an opportunity to restate his policy. Those who wanted only easy and uncontroversial articles were mistaken. Readers should be prepared to tackle thoughtful pieces about difficult problems, provided that a fair balance was kept over the articles in general.

In 1985 Mike Canny became editor, and again the style (and the cover!) changed. Unfortunately he was advised to resign after four years because of ill-health. Under the watchful eye of this 'thoroughly competent editor' the circulation rapidly increased, as did the number of pages, and a wider range of articles was published. Now the editorship has passed to Dr Carole Cull, who also promises a stimulating and lively magazine judging by her first issues – and her own lively personality.

Compulsive reading?

At first sight it might appear that since 1904 the impact of *The Reader* on the Church of England has been negligible. That would be an injustice. Now at its best in almost ninety years, the magazine has helped Readers towards a better understanding of their faith and has given them practical support in communicating it to others. At its worst it has been a very dull news-sheet, to be glanced through in an idle moment and then tossed aside.

What should Readers expect? Where are the cartoonists and the graphic artists among the Readers? Today, Readers' understanding of the Christian faith is found along a continuum from radical through liberal and conservative to fundamentalist. How might we deal more effectively with controversial matters in *The Reader*? As representatives of the laity, more than 99 per cent of the Church, what have we to say to one another, and what have we to say that the clergy and the whole Church need to hear? *The Reader* belongs to Readers, and with the increasing professionalism of its editors and contributors over the years, perhaps it is time to consider the contribution which *The Reader* might make to the Church as a whole. How might *The*

Reader grow to stand alongside *Theology, The Modern Churchman,* and *Anvil* in forming and interpreting faith, not only among Readers but among other Christians? How might Readers be encouraged to bring together their professional expertise, theological understanding and faith in the struggle to discern and express Christian values in the world, and to share them with the whole Church?

10: Opening Reader ministry to women

> A lay person, whether man or woman, who is baptised and confirmed and who satisfies the bishop that he is a regular communicant of the Church of England may be admitted by the bishop of the diocese to the office of reader in the Church and licensed by him to perform any duty or duties which may lawfully be performed by a reader . . .

By these words of Canon E4 *Of Readers*, the ministry of women Readers was introduced on 7 May 1969, just over a hundred years after the revival of the office of Reader. By the end of 1969 there were nine women Readers; by 1979, over 500 and by 1989, nearly 2,000. While the number of women continues to increase, the number of men has shown a slight decline since 1969. Women Readers share their ministry alongside male colleagues without differentiation of role or function, but because they often are or have been the first *women* to exercise a *preaching* ministry in their parishes, their perception of their experience as Readers may differ in significant ways from that of men.

Women in the Church of England in the nineteenth century

While the frustration of Florence Nightingale, who was told by the Church authorities to 'go home and do your crochet', arouses the sympathy of many women in the Church today, it left most of her contemporaries mystified. Yet throughout the nineteenth century, despite male opposition, a few able and determined women were creating a space for themselves and their successors within the Church of England. The first woman missionary from the Church Missionary Society set sail in 1820, and the first from the Society for the Propagation of the Gospel in 1857. Service in the mission field remained one of the very few openings for women who felt God was calling them into full-time service in the Church. From 1845 a woman might join one of the religious communities which were being founded, often for the relief of poor and sick people in homes at the opposite end of the social scale from which most of the sisters were drawn.

In 1862 Bishop Tait of London ordained the first deaconess of modern times in the Church of England. No one at that time, and for the century which followed, was quite sure whether deaconesses were in Holy Orders, or whether they were just a holy order which was not quite clergy and not quite laity either. In a debate on the diaconate in the Convocation of Canterbury in 1884 a member of the Lower House enquired whether 'females' were included in the Resolution, only to be told firmly that deaconesses were not within the Committee's terms of reference. Nevertheless it was a fair question.

In 1887 Church Army sisters began work as lay evangelists. By 1889 some thirty to forty women were working among women in Liverpool, besides several hundred who were voluntarily involved in Sunday school teaching. By 1901, out of every hundred Anglicans, 65 were women. For many of these women, most of whom were married with families, the Mothers' Union offered support and fostered a sense of responsibility for the religious upbringing of children. From its origins in 1876 when Mary Sumner organized a meeting for 'cottage mothers and lady mothers' in her husband's parish of Old Alresford, the Mothers' Union (as it became known) quickly grew and spread to other dioceses.

While a few women were sincerely seeking for ways to express their commitment to God in the service of the Church in the world, most women and men would have concurred with the Bishop of London who, at the Diocesan Conference in 1914, declared that women may give addresses from the chancel steps. That was as far as public opinion allowed them to go, for 'the great mass of women in England were opposed to other women haranguing mixed congregations in Church'. Incidentally, his choice of words is interesting. Was he meaning to associate 'giving addresses' with 'haranguing'? If so, how might his words have related to the experience of 'mixed congregations' listening to men, clerical and lay, speaking in church? Or was the Bishop confusing the few women permitted to speak in church with the suffragettes in the streets outside? While they are unlikely to have been the same women, it is just possible that they might have been moved by the same Gospel!

The opening of Reader ministry to women
In the very first issue of *The Reader and Lay Worker* an editorial note recorded that it was

a matter for regret that our first number is written throughout by the sterner sex so called. Women's work and influence are so great that we should be indeed neglecting a plain duty if we did not enlist the services of those who are doing the one and exercising the other.

In 1920 the Lambeth Conference resolved that laywomen should be given the same opportunity as laymen to speak and pray in consecrated buildings at non-statutory services. The following year the Bishop of Wakefield raised the question of women Readers in the Convocation of York but no action was taken. On a more mundane level, perhaps the publication of a review of a book entitled *We Women: A Golden Hope* in *The Lay Reader* in 1924 reflects the real attitude of at least some Readers towards women, and indicates the great gap which had to be bridged before women's ministry might be accepted on the same terms as that of men:

> This book would make a quite suitable textbook for a short Church Tutorial Class on the psychology of woman. It is nicely written and readable by all. There is a distinctly feminine ring about it without anything effeminate. For those who want sermons on the question of women, the writer has provided a dozen with texts and nice poetic endings ... The outlook is very deeply Christian ... Again and again one comes across short sentences which mean so much. In the chapter on 'Our Strength', we get, for example, 'conduct founded on ignorance is never wise or safe'.

The first major advance towards the ministry of women Readers was taken in *The Ministry of Women*, a report of an Archbishops' Commission in 1935, set up 'to examine any theological or other relevant principles which have governed or ought to govern the Church in the development of the Ministry of Women'. Its report recommended that there should be a trained woman on the staff of every important parish. More than fifty years later this has still to be achieved. It affirmed

> that Christian principles require that the Church should secure for women as full opportunities and scope for the exercise of their characteristic gifts and capacities in its ministry as it secures for men in the exercise of theirs ...
>
> Lay women should be eligible for such offices and duties in the Church as are open to lay men, *including that of Lay Reader*; that authority should be given to some to preach, to take occasional services and to conduct retreats ... and that in each

diocese there should be women qualified by training in theology to give lectures and advanced teaching. (My italics)

The report was primarily concerned with improving the status and function of both deaconesses and licensed lay workers, most of whom were poorly paid and given very limited recognition. Thus the report recommended that they should be allowed to preach and take such services as may be taken by laymen. Hence it was a logical extension that the office of Reader should be open to women.

But action was slow. In 1939, during the debate on *The Work and Status of Readers* report, a clergyman in the Convocation of Canterbury queried the assumption that all Readers should be male. Three years later Dr Murray wrote that the main function of the office of Reader was to witness to the prophethood of the laity, and that there had been from the beginning women as well as men endowed with the prophetic gift. Central Readers' Board, however, decided the matter was 'too intricate' to be discussed in wartime! They were not allowed to escape so easily!

The Central Council for Women's Church Work sent a memorandum to CRB enquiring why the 1935 recommendations had not been implemented, and, more specifically, whether CRB had any objections in principle. If there were no objections, they wondered whether CRB considered it 'undesirable at the present time on grounds of expediency', and if so, whether individual bishops might license a few well-qualified women to do the work of Readers without the status of Readers and under a different name.

The discussion which followed did CRB little credit. It was claimed that the inclusion of women would prejudice the whole cause, and that women could already help in other spheres such as Sunday school and home visiting. A sub-committee was set up and its report circulated to Diocesan Readers' Boards. In effect it abandoned all responsibility, for 'while regarding the work of women in the Church with admiration and thankfulness', it thought the principle should be decided by the whole Church. Furthermore, as there appeared to be no sign of any need or general demand, either on the part of the laity or of the majority of women Church workers, they considered women should not be admitted to the office of Reader. As far as Readers were concerned the matter was allowed to rest, but the Central Council for Women's Church Work rightly continued to press for a better deal for licensed lay workers.

The next major development was a debate in the Church Assembly in 1959 requesting Convocation 'to consider so amending draft Canon 91 as to provide that a woman may be admitted as a Reader'. This was significant in that Reader ministry was to be regulated by Canon and thus brought right into the ecclesiastical system. The debate reflected the main arguments of the time.

Those who opposed the motion claimed that it raised suspicion, fear and prejudice; that it departed from age-long tradition of the Church; that it would hinder reunion; that there was insufficient evidence in the New Testament to justify it; and that it was a matter for the whole Church.

Those who supported it called attention to the position of women in medicine, the law and commerce and maintained that 'it was only in the Church that the shackle of sex prejudice crippled their efforts'. There was no justification for the Church continuing to treat laymen and laywomen differently in their opportunities for service. Were women fellow-members of the laity with men, or were they, by the accident of birth, not really members of the Church at all? Modern, intellectual people on the fringe of the Church could not understand the Church's rigid and out-of-date attitude toward the admission of women. The Church was not only losing the services of those who could serve as Readers, but was alienating from active membership women of distinction and education in other spheres of life. Though the motion was carried in Church Assembly, it was another ten years before women became Readers.

In 1962 the report *Gender and Ministry* was prepared for Church Assembly by the recently formed Central Advisory Council for Training and Ministry in consultation with the new Council for Women's Ministry in the Church. While it was mainly concerned with the recruitment and use of women for full-time service in the Church, it pleaded for a reinterpretation of the laity's share in the life, worship and witness of the Church. The Appendices provide a useful indication of the extent of women's ministry in the Church in 1960 and help to put the call for women Readers into the context of women's ministry as a whole. There are 1,501 members of religious communities; 469 moral welfare workers; 446 licensed lay workers; 261 Church Army sisters and 65 deaconesses in full-time Church work.

The debate which followed was sympathetic towards women Readers and Convocation was requested to implement the 1935 report. In the Convocation of Canterbury, Readers themselves were criticized. They had become 'archaic'; they obstructed the ministry of the laity; they should become part-time priests or deacons. There was greater encouragement, however, for the possibility of women Readers: if a Reader was a representative layman, surely a woman was no less representative of the whole laity in worship; there was 'a considerable number of educated women who could serve the

Church as Readers . . . a good deal more effectively than some clergy and some Readers because they were well trained . . . and some held degrees in theology'.

It cannot be said that CRB facilitated the admission of women Readers in any way. It failed to follow up the 1935 Archbishops' Commission and took no steps to implement it. When approached by the Central Council for Women's Church Work, it was evasive and missed a golden opportunity to educate the Church into the wider opportunities of lay ministry, preferring to pass responsibility for decision-making on to the Church as a whole, without offering it the benefit of its own extensive experience. It failed to extend a hand of friendship to the licensed lay workers who were fighting battles which Readers had already won. Worse still, it completely under-estimated the contribution which women were already making to the ministry of the laity, and failed to appreciate the frustration of those women whose spirituality, allied to theological and professional quali-fications, already fitted them for Reader ministry. Perhaps some of them feared that those women were too well qualified for Readership!

CRB did, however, make one very positive contribution. It insisted that if or when women were admitted to the office of Reader it should be done upon the same terms and under the same regulations and controls as for men. This has proved of lasting benefit to the Reader movement – not that women Readers would have wanted it otherwise.

One amusing incident occurred in the mid-1960s while the dis-cussions were continuing. It was discovered that a woman had actu-ally passed the General Readers' Examination! Apparently she had attended classes provided under the aegis of the London County Council and therefore open to the public, and had entered for the examination as part of a block entry. In February 1965 CRB charac-teristically declared that it had no power to accept entries from women, and provided separate entry forms with space for full Christ-ian names! Six months later the Board agreed that women should be immediately eligible to sit General Readers' Examination, if (not when!) Royal Assent was given to the proposed Canon.

When women were finally admitted in 1969 the CRB seems to have accepted the inevitable without comment. The first woman to attend a meeting of CRB was Miss D. S. Chalk, who substituted for one of the representatives from the Diocese of Carlisle at the Annual General Meeting in March 1973. York diocese sent the first elected woman member, Mrs E. D. Hanson. In 1981, when I attended my first Central Readers' Conference I was one of three women representatives – and we were addressed as 'brethren' throughout

the weekend! There are now approximately twenty women representatives on Central Readers' Conference; and all Readers have ben-
efitted from the dignity and wisdom which Mrs Hilda Flint brought
to her duties as Vice-Chair from 1985 to 1990.

Correspondence in *The Reader* on the topic of women Readers
might be considered predictable and reflected the editor's own attitude by the choice of such headings as 'Adam and Eve'. Two positive
approaches stand out. The first from a Reader in April 1964:

> One of the great virtues of admitting women as Readers would
> be to allow us all, those who agree and those who think there
> *are* theological objections, to get used psychologically to the idea
> of women leading morning and evening prayer and as occasion
> arises, administering the Chalice. This would then give us a real
> opportunity over the years to have the experience on which to
> base a judgement on the much more vexed question of ordination
> of women to the priesthood . . . there never has been a case for
> any differentiation whatever between laymen and laywomen in
> their offices in the Church, other than social conventions and
> prevailing psychological attitudes to them.

A year later, when the Anglican–Methodist Conversations were
taking place, another Reader pointed out that the Methodist Church
used lay people

> not just for the chores of Church life, but in the day to day work
> and witness of the Church, in speaking and preaching . . . The
> place of women in the office of Reader is one of right and not of
> need and expediency.

The writer of the editorial notes was obviously not welcoming to
women. He greeted the notice in the Gazette of the first woman
Reader, Miss D. M. Chant, BD, with the comment:

> Winchester appears to be the first diocese to admit a woman as
> Reader. History does not relate how she was dressed . . . She was
> given a diocesan licence so it would appear that no particular
> parish is to enjoy her ministry.

And in July 1970 he drew attention to the one or two dioceses where
women, with the approval of their bishops, unfortunately decided
not to adopt the regulation uniform of cassock, surplice, blue scarf,
and hood if appropriate.

> Competition is breaking out between dioceses in an attempt to
> find the most attractive dress for women Readers . . . It will be

interesting to note the diocese which succeeds in designing a costume farthest removed from the sobriety and dignity of cassock and surplice.

Considering that it took male Readers almost a hundred years before they were identically clothed, the comment was ungallant to say the least!

As for the *Church Times*, the only mention of the Canon allowing women to become Readers was tucked away in a column by Rosamund Essex, after two paragraphs on not wearing hats in church. As a former editor of the *Church Times* for ten years, Rosamund Essex's own licensing merited one paragraph of 'Pennyfields' journal under the title of 'Ladies at the Lectern'.

Who were the first women Readers?

Licensed as Readers in the first year or so were professional women with theological qualifications, because they were already there, trained and waiting. A few already had their bishop's permission to speak in Church until such time as women might become Readers. Now, over twenty years on, the background of women Readers is a diverse as that of men. Many are in full- or part-time employment in almost every kind of work. Others are housewives, often with varied interests and responsibilities in the life of the local community. Some are clergy wives who want to be more closely involved with their husband's work, and to use their spiritual and intellectual gifts within the parish. There are a few members of religious communities who value the training and opportunities offered through Reader ministry. In dioceses where there are pastoral assistants or pastoral workers, some have exercised a ministry which has led them to seek the wider opportunities of a preaching ministry, together with the authorization to take funerals as an extension of work which they have already been doing with the dying and bereaved. As with men, some Readers in the early years of their retirement are virtually unpaid curates in their parishes.

At first women Readers were regarded with mild curiosity, especially when visiting beyond their own parish. It seems strange now to think that one of the questions I was asked most often was 'What do you wear?' My reply was always 'The same as the men'. This was usually followed by 'What do you wear on your head?' to which I again replied 'The same as the men' and waited for their reaction.

In some parishes the first women Readers had a hard time. One, the first in her diocese, had the full approval of her vicar and PCC when she started training, but when she was licensed there was consternation amongst the congregation. One of the men declared that if a woman got up in the pulpit he would leave the church. And a woman with 40 years' experience as a Sunday school teacher said 'I've nothing against you, dear, but you see it was through a woman that sin came into the world and I don't think a woman should preach.' This was hard for the Reader, and for her vicar, whom she described as 'caught like someone who had dipped his toe into the water and was hopping about because it was so cold'. This Reader has worked under two priests who have done all they can to give her responsibility, though one is against and the other in favour of the ordination of women.

Most women Readers find that, provided they exercise their public ministry with reasonable competence, they are quickly accepted, and many fears and prejudices are overcome. Many women feel affirmed by hearing a woman's voice leading the service; a few will still avoid a woman Reader offering the chalice. One Church, which had refused to recommend a laywoman for the bishop's authorization to administer the chalice, on the grounds that women could not serve in the sanctuary, found itself with a woman Reader who had moved from another diocese. The vicar gave her a warm welcome, and within a year or so the parish had women lay assistants and servers as well as men. Once people are used to seeing and hearing a woman Reader in church, their usual comment about women's ministry is that they wonder what all the fuss is about. Experience also shows that the ministry of one woman, be she Reader, deacon, deaconess, Church Army sister or accredited lay worker, makes it much easier for her successors.

11: Women as Readers

A preaching ministry

Two organizations, other than Church Army and the Salvation Army, for many years prepared the way for women Readers as preachers. The first was the Women's World Day of Prayer, which annually draws together at least half a million women – and men too – in England and Wales as participants in an international day of prayer based on a service prepared by women from a different part of the world every year. The significance of this movement for local ecumenical relations and for the ministry of women has never received its due recognition in Anglican circles. Yet it has done more than any other movement to encourage women to worship together in one another's churches without anxiety, often using forms of worship and prayer which are new to the participants. It has also given women the opportunity to exercise leadership roles and to speak in church.

The second organization is the Mothers' Union, which, while it cannot speak for all Anglican women, has tried to move with the times despite opposition from some of its own members on occasions. The Mothers' Union has worked hard to train women as speakers and give them much encouragement. The involvement of a very large number of clergy wives, particularly in the past, assured the Mothers' Union an established place in the life of the Church of England, so that able and articulate diocesan presidents and other officers and members have been welcomed as an asset rather than viewed as a threat. So the way was being prepared, at least in some areas, for women Readers as preachers.

There can be no doubt that some women Readers have a theological understanding, depth of spiritual insight and necessary skills of communication to be good, able preachers. For at least three-quarters of the congregation sitting in the pews, it can be a relief to have images drawn from human experience other than cricket and trains! The truth is that congregations are enriched by preaching which is shared between women and men, clerical and lay, undergirded by the prayer of the whole people of God.

Almost all Readers, women and men, take considerable trouble to ensure that their sermons, addresses, prayers and intercessions are appropriate both to their congregations and to the occasion. Language is living: we absorb new words (like *glasnost*), discard old ones (like 'quick', meaning 'living'), give some (like 'gay') new meanings. Conventions which have served well in the past are no longer acceptable to many people, and words like 'men' and 'mankind' can no longer be used to denote all human beings. In any congregation there are likely to be people with different perceptions of what is, and what is not, acceptable usage, but an increasing number of men and women feel alienated by the use of exclusive language.

While the Alternative Service Book claims that 'Christians are formed by the way in which they pray, and the way they choose to pray expresses what they are', the Liturgical Commission chose to ignore the promptings of its two women members (one of whom is a Reader with extensive experience in the World Council of Churches), to incorporate inclusive language. All Readers have an opportunity to make a significant contribution to the life and understanding of the whole Church by habitually using inclusive language, not only in liturgy and preaching, but also in PCCs, committees and synods. Much can be achieved by light-hearted banter, but this is not just a passing fad of the few. Underneath is a serious pleading for a Christ-like sensitivity and awareness which accords to all the human dignity which we claim for ourselves.

A pastoral ministry

While in essence there is no difference between the ministry of men or women Readers there are certain areas where women seem particularly gifted, and are able to use their experience to contribute to their work as preachers, pastors and conductors of funerals. While there are some grandfatherly Readers who run superb crèches from time to time, some women are very successful with pram services and similar activities. For example, one Reader in a village meets other mothers outside the infants' school, and from initial contacts the mothers have brought friends, and friends of friends, most of whom had little or no contact with the Church. Some fifty women are now involved. At the other end of life, an elderly Reader who happens to be disabled, and walks with a frame, regularly takes a service in the local old people's home, where her age and infirmity make for an immediate common understanding.

Many women find themselves involved in pastoral ministry of

various kinds, including baptismal preparation. A few serve as part-time chaplain's assistants in local hospitals, either permanently or between appointments. The chaplain's interest and support can lead to a ministry which is both challenging and rewarding. Another creative time for ministry development can be an interregnum. One Reader, then aged 72, worked in partnership with a non-stipendiary minister who lived several miles away and was only able to function at weekends. She did all the baptismal preparation, conducted three or four funerals a week, preached every Sunday, and once in an emergency due to sudden illness, and with the permission of the Rural Dean, took three baptisms. She was 'virtually the vicar of the parish from Monday to Friday', all with the help of a husband in the background doing the household chores.

Some women Readers find themselves taking funerals quite regularly, including those which occur on the vicar's day off. Other funerals are taken because the Readers have already drawn close to the family concerned through visiting the dying. Occasionally a family will not accept a woman Reader, though whether this is due to her being a woman or a layperson is unclear. Usually the feedback is more positive, especially among those who were initially shocked by the appearance of a woman at the beginning of a service. Women may bring 'sympathy, ability, conscientiousness, an attention to detail – and – this is the big bonus – men feel they can cry in your presence and not lose face', writes one experienced Reader. I suspect that, in proportion to their numbers, women take more funerals than men – though it must be remembered that in some dioceses the bishop has yet to give Readers, men and women alike, permission to take funerals, even after specific training to do so.

Care and counselling ministries are a special concern of some women Readers, together with a healing ministry including the laying-on of hands. Having time for people is much appreciated, especially by those too sensitive and undemanding to approach a 'busy vicar'. Where a woman's ministry has been rejected, there may be a very painful ministry of reconciliation, to minister God's love and healing in so far as that may be permitted. Some women are led into the field of spiritual guidance and the conducting of retreats, which one describes as 'so much a nurturing of life, baptismal life'. Not all ministry is giving; some of the most fruitful happens when the minister learns to receive the ministry of others.

Some husbands and wives are able to offer a ministry in partnership which is much appreciated. Two doctors who became Readers worked closely together; one would take the service and the other would preach. After several years they retired to a rural area which had lost three out of four incumbents in the previous five years. When the husband was eventually ordained as a non-stipendiary minister, the wife shared in the Communion service as far as she was able.

After my husband's death I had many letters saying how much this shared ministry was appreciated. We were seen as a team working together, planning together and ministering together. We represented Christian marriage and Christian family life and we were viewed as real down to earth people who had worked together in medicine and now worked together in Christian witness and worship. It seems that this united living witness was more important than anything we ever said in sermons.

A prophetic ministry

Women no less than men are called to a prophetic ministry, both in society and in the Church. The call to witness to a faith which lives with questions rather than answers is not easily shared among congregations who have been encouraged to look for certainty, security and a peaceful existence, rather than the risks and adventures of a pilgrim journey. Just because the structures of the Church of England are male-dominated, so women Readers – perhaps more so than men – are called to a prophetic ministry within the organization as members of Synods and their committees. For some professional women who are used to making their points which stand or fall on their merits, it comes as an unwelcome shock to realize that in Church circles some points are heard only in relation to the gender of those who make them, and that there are times when the substance of one's arguments is better presented by one's male colleagues. Men are said to speak 'from conviction'; a woman making the same point in the same way is labelled 'strident'!

Until the priesthood of women is fully accepted and they have won recognition as clergy colleagues on equal terms, women Readers have a specific role to call attention to the ministry and witness of the *whole people of God*. As laypeople they can speak out on women's issues and draw attention to occasions when women's interests and skills, whether lay or diaconal, should be called upon. The composition of committees and agendas, the decision-making processes and their implications, must all be subject to scrutiny and comment if women are to live in the Church in partnership with men, using their gifts to the full. Such a ministry may well be painful, lonely and dispiriting, but there will always be some, both clergy and lay, who will voice their support, not during the debates but afterwards in private.

On a happier note, there are many women Readers who are making an outstanding contribution to the wider Church. Dr Christina Baxter, for example, was one of three members of the Church of England who recently took part in a Partners in Mission consultation for the Church in the Province of Southern Africa. Jean Mayland, a Reader at York Minster, has had an important role in both the British and the World Councils of Churches, and is also President of the Ecumenical Forum of European Christian Women. Both have been able to share their insights from these wider experiences of the Church through their Reader ministry in preaching, speaking, and not least through their articles in *The Reader* and elsewhere.

As an illustration of a prophetic ministry in society I quote from a community care worker involved with people with severe mental health problems.

> I see ministry in terms of the dialogue which I can initiate between what the Gospel has to say and people's own experience . . . These young homeless men and women have profound insights into what it means to be human, and where God might be and why suffering is. Essentially, they are 'doing theology' at the sharp end of life. The Church needs their unique experience, and they need the acceptance of a community . . . Reader ministry is not confined to what goes on in Church, nor even in the parish. Most of my ministry takes place in my work setting which is outside both. Reader ministry is about the giving of all that one is. People and God and Society are so interconnected that one cannot have dealings with one in isolation.
>
> I like the idea that God lets us be. I want to follow that way, the way that encourages, promotes discovery, supports growth, speaks up on our behalf, protects our freedom of choice. This sort of love neither suffocates nor alienates. It attracts people without restricting their space. It acts respectfully. Love like this makes us glad to be alive. Once we know that love like this exists, we want there to be more of it around. And we want its tenets of justice, compassion, respect to be self-evident in the ordering of our society and the social policies of our day . . .
>
> I find myself challenging the social policies of this country at least as often as I lead worship on a Sunday. I would not be doing one without the other. It's the experience of God's love that fuels my desire for social justice and my ministry as a Reader. (Teresa Parker)

Prophetic ministries make it impossible to draw boundaries between what is done as a Reader in Church and in the rest of life. Such ministries can be costly and painful. But they also offer grace and freedom to be and to enable others to be.

Limitations

It would be dishonest to pretend that women Readers are always welcomed with open arms. Here and there a few women deacons seem so unsure of their own positions that they are nervous of other women with a liturgical and preaching ministry. Other laywomen may also regard a woman Reader as a threat in the sense that their own service to the Church may *appear* to be devalued. A sensitive woman Reader will quickly realize the need to affirm everyone's contribution to the maintenance of the life of the Church and the coming of the Kingdom of God. Some women Readers find themselves patronized by men, particularly in synods and committees, at least until they have become established in their role. More difficult to accommodate are those clergy who believe strongly in the headship of the male, and that all women are subordinate to male authority.

A change of incumbent can be more difficult for women than for men Readers. While some clergy will respect a man with theological, teaching or pastoral gifts, a woman with identical gifts may well be viewed as a threat rather than as a resource available to the parish. Much prayer, patience and good will is called for to establish good working relationships in such circumstances. On the other hand, an able Reader may well hold a parish together when ordained staff are found wanting.

Moving to another diocese may also be a critical time for both men and women Readers, but especially for a woman if she moves to a parish which has not experienced women's ministry. The incumbent of the new parish may choose to ignore a newly-arrived Reader for weeks, even months, leaving her no alternative but to find another parish where her services will be acceptable. Or again, the circumstances in the parish itself may change when, for example, an incumbent divides a congregation and threatens its very life. At such a time a woman Reader may become particularly vulnerable and in need of support as well as giving appropriate support as the 'plot . . . twists and unfolds' (see James Hopewell, *Congregation*, SCM Press, 1988).

Considering that women Readers have only been licensed since 1969, the negative aspects of their work might have loomed much more ominously than appears at present. Most owe a great debt to their clergy, their parishes and their Reader colleagues. In one diocese, the bishop retired just months after licensing the first woman Reader. The minor canon who was marshalling the procession for the farewell service looked quite confused when the woman appeared. He began to direct her towards the women lay workers and deaconesses, only to be faced with a chorus of Readers saying firmly 'She's one of us'. Happily, that is the experience of the majority.

Women Readers and feminist theology

The earliest women Readers stepped into a male world. It was dominated by male clergy, with here and there a deaconess or licensed lay worker giving sterling, but often taken-for-granted, service without any recognized place in the system. Though women Readers quickly gained acceptance among their male colleagues there was an indefinable pressure to conform. In many parishes support for the ordination of women was affirmed, even encouraged, but the much larger issues relating to feminist theology were – and still are – considered so extreme as to be beyond the pale. When pressed, few Readers – men or women – are able to give a coherent account of feminist theology and most simply do not want to know.

Most church people take for granted the tradition which has been preserved and interpreted in the Church, largely by men for men, within prevailing cultures. Christian feminists have found a new richness by exploring the 'silent' tradition, which is in the Bible and Christian tradition, but which has been passed over by a patriarchal society and a patriarchal Church. It is not just a question of whether God is 'Mother' as well as 'Father', but that God is beyond all gender and *equally* available to *all* human beings.

For example, the stories of Sarah, Miriam, Deborah and Ruth resonate in new ways with women's experience in our own time. Similarly Jesus' encounters with women as recorded in the Gospels show him breaking through contemporary cultural and religious conventions, and affirming their calling to healing and wholeness of body, mind and spirit. This renewed understanding of Jesus' relations with women is helping many women to explore their own experiences and to perceive that *all* experiences are open to the love of God. Whereas the tradition emphasizes a God who is almighty, all-powerful and sovereign, feminists redress the balance by drawing attention to the God who suffers with and through the Son in abandonment on the cross, thus revealing the depth of suffering love seen in God.

It follows, therefore, that many women are revaluing the feminine in human life, including the life of the Church. They are no longer content to be second-class Christians, circumscribed by male conventions and male decision-making. This is not a negative challenge to the structures of the Church, but a new, positive vision of the Body of Christ, a Body which values *all* its members, men and women, in a sharing of differences and complementarity through worship, life, witness and organization. Thus feminist theology helps all of us to enlarge our understanding of God, humanity and the Church through expressions of wholeness and unity.

Feminist theologians will continue to challenge the Church, not necessarily in a confrontational way, but through the development of the tradition. Some, in anger and frustration, will exclude themselves from the Church's life and thinking and leave the Church behind. Others, at some cost to themselves, will stay within the Church as witnesses to newly-revealed truth. I believe it is time for women Readers to show a greater awareness of, and more openness towards, feminist theology. Some individuals already participate in groups such as Women in Theology and the Ecumenical Forum of Christian Women. They worship through experimental liturgies, and explore their experiences with other like-minded (and at times not so like-minded!) women in supportive groups. But as far as I am aware they form a very small proportion of active women Readers.

Both men and women Readers need to create more opportunities to explore and interpret feminist theology, and to contribute to its development as lay ministers. For some, working out feminist insights will call for painful and often isolating activity within the structures of the Church. Such is the present climate of opinion that all need wisdom in discerning the time to speak and the time to suffer in silence.

Women Readers and the Church's ministry

What have women Readers achieved? Their growth in numbers has been remarkable and they now form about a quarter of the total number of Readers. They are increasingly taking their share in the organizing of Reader ministry as diocesan officers. The diocese of Rochester is proud to have the first woman Reader, Mrs Sarah James, to be appointed Warden, though she is not the first woman Warden. The present editor of *The Reader*, Dr Carole Cull, is a former Diocesan Secretary. For the first time CRC's Annual General Meeting in 1990 elected more women than men members to its Executive Committee.

Women are regularly exercising a preaching, liturgical, teaching and pastoral ministry in the Church. Quite apart from the quality of the ministry which they may by God's grace offer, their regular service 'up front' is an encouragement to other women who might feel called to ministry, ordained or lay. They also help to allay the fears of those opposed to the ordination of women to the priesthood, especially as they fulfil their duties in the sanctuary and administer the bread and the cup at Holy Communion. Most women Readers will have met members of their congregation who have commented that in the past they have been opposed to the ordination of women, but that now they have experienced the ministry of women they have changed their mind. The appearance of women Readers as visiting ministers or preachers in parishes other than their own, and the sight of women taking their part in processions at deanery and diocesan services, again reinforces the normality of women and men in partnership. In these and other ways, women Readers are also working alongside women deacons towards a time when the Church will give full recognition to the gifts of all its women, ordained and lay.

Some women Readers are very sensitive to the feelings and needs of women who serve the Church in other ways, as flower-arrangers, coffee-makers, churchwardens, PCC secretaries and treasurers, and the host of other tasks which help the community to build up its corporate life. A sensitive woman Reader affirm the gifts of *all* members of the Church, and claims no special status for herself. Indeed it is often by working *alongside* other members of the congregation that she makes contact and befriends those in need, both within the fellowship and with those with no previous experience of the Church. Hence she is often able to work 'on the fringe' where clergy might have greater difficulty in making initial contacts. Similarly, professional women may also develop their ministry outside the parish as opportunities arise.

'Women think and work and feel differently from men, and there is considerable deprivation for both sexes in a parish where ministry is conceived and vested solely in the ordained man', wrote one of my correspondents. There is now an increasing number of parishes where ministry is *shared* among men and women, ordained and lay. Women Readers affirm their *lay* status, often working alongside women deacons to prepare the way, on the one hand, for the ordination of women to the priesthood, and on the other, for a more fulfilling discipleship for all women – and men. This is a significant contribution to our understanding of ministry within the Church of England, yet one which is often overlooked and undervalued. The Church needs the gifts of *all* its members.

12: Readers and Other Ministers

Because all human beings are made in the image of God, they are called to become the People of God, the Church, servants and ministers and citizens of the Kingdom, a new humanity in Jesus Christ. Though we are tainted by our sinfulness, God's wonderful grace and love offer us all this common Christian vocation. God leaves everyone free to refuse this call; but the call is there for all without exception. ('The Common Statement', *All Are Called*, CIO Publishing, 1985)

While the Church of England accepts in theory that 'all are called', it finds it very difficult to work it out in practice. Much is said about 'the People of God' being laity and clergy together, but it is a partnership which is at best elusive, and at worst non-existent. Although clergy make up less than one per cent of the People of God, they dominate the life of most parishes, and in effect control the synodical structures of Church government. Yet the laity themselves need to explore their discipleship more imaginatively and faithfully, and live out their calling in more positive ways. Readers, as laypeople with theological training, are significantly poised to explore more deeply the meaning of 'all are called' as it might be worked out in Church and society today, as clergy and laity walk together on the pilgrim way.

Blurring the boundaries

The last twenty years or so have seen a proliferation of lay ministries within the Church of England. Pastoral workers, pastoral assistants, elders, counsellors, administrators, community and youth workers, musicians, as well as churchwardens, PCC secretaries and treasurers, all in their different ways assist the clergy in their parochial work. They are not all found in every parish, nor in every diocese.

Anyone invited by the incumbent may read the lessons or lead the intercessions, and churchwardens are expected to read Morning or Evening Prayer (apart from the absolution) in the unavoidable absence of a priest or Reader. In many dioceses, bishops give permission to a limited number of lay people to assist with the chalice, usually for a period of one to three years, and at the request of the incumbent and PCC. An increasing number of laymen and laywomen, especially those who have gifts of music, drama and dance, are becoming actively involved in the liturgy, A few take an active part in services of laying-on of hands and of healing, and in some parishes lay people preach without the bishop's authorization. Thus alongside Readers many lay people are actively involved in church services.

Many dioceses now have voluntary pastoral assistants or pastoral workers, men and women who, after training, have been authorized by the bishop to assist the clergy in the pastoral work of the parish. Their duties may include home and hospital visiting, baptismal visits and preparation, and taking Communion to the housebound. Normally their work depends on the needs of the parish, the time they have available, their personal gifts and possibly professional skills, and their initial and continuing training. Some may have a flair for working with young families, others with the dying and bereaved, and others with drug-users or the homeless. Pastoral assistants or workers may take part in church services but they are not licensed to preach.

A few dioceses have lay elders who share with the clergy in the leadership and pastoral care of the parish. They too are authorized to work within the parish at the request of the incumbent and the PCC. Like the pastoral workers they may also take part in church services but they are not licensed to preach. Their training varies from diocese to diocese; often they receive very little. There is no doubt, however, that elders and pastoral assistants or workers exercise a ministry which is well blessed and highly valued in their respective parishes, and without which the Church would be much poorer.

The growth of authorized lay ministries in many dioceses raises questions for Readers and for the Church in general. Must all who undertake specific forms of service be labelled and authorized? Are we creating two classes of Christians, some authorized and some not? Are we in danger of stifling and diminishing those who do good by stealth in neighbourly acts of kindness, or by listening to other people's troubles, or encouraging young and old along the Way? Are we implying that the housebound of all ages, or those with limited time, have no ministry worth recognizing and affirming? Is it not time, therefore, that instead of emphasizing 'lay ministries' we recovered and used the word 'discipleship' and made it work in the Gospel senses of 'learning' and 'following Jesus' – for everyone, clergy and laity together?

Readers cannot escape these questions, especially if they are to continue exercising an authorized lay ministry of preaching and teaching within a pastoral context. In the past, and still in some quarters, Readers have been defensive and ungracious as more lay people have taken part in the liturgy by assisting with the chalice, reading lessons, leading intercessions, and in other ways. Some Readers have not found it easy to stand down from customary duties for which they have been trained, while others take over with greater or lesser expertise. Yet increasing participation by the laity offers real opportunities for Readers to share their ministry, to affirm and enable other members of the congregation and to learn from them if they will.

In some parishes there is a danger of lay ministers becoming too church-centred. Some lay people spend most of their time ministering to other lay people within the church fellowship. Many of those outside the church with more pressing needs are left in the cold. Readers have an opportunity to turn the focus outward. Some may choose to do this by seeing what people have it in them to do, and working alongside them to encourage them to use their gifts; others by focussing their own ministry almost wholly within the community rather than the church. A wise church will always be looking outwards, upholding all its 'ministers' in prayer, wherever and however they are called to serve.

Readers and ordained ministers

In recent years the number of Readers admitted has been greater than the number of ministers ordained. In some dioceses there are more Readers than clergy. In 1945 almost all ordained ministers had parochial appointments or were serving as chaplains in HM Forces. A few worked in schools and universities. In the 1990s the clergy have a much wider range of options. While the great majority still serve as parish clergy, some are employed full-time (or part-time in joint parish or cathedral appointments) in 'sector' ministries such as education, industrial mission or social responsibility. Others become hospital, prison or Forces chaplains.

Since 1960 an increasing number have trained in part-time courses to become non-stipendiary ministers (NSMs). Some NSMs have retired from secular employment and work virtually full-time for the Church without payment. Most NSMs continue in full-time secular employment, but the thrust of their ministry is in the parish rather than at work. Within a few years of ordination more than a third transfer to full-time stipendiary ministry.

Another group of ordained ministers have recently been recognized as ministers in secular employment (MSEs). These have usually trained as NSMs and see their secular employment as the focus of their ministry. Though attached to a parish as their base they may not be much involved in its day-to-day life.

> Ministers in Secular Employment continue to work in secular contexts, because they can see signs of God's presence there as well as within the Church. They need skills of discernment and prophetic insight, as they reflect theologically on the corporate and personal realities. They have a task, within the Church, of enabling people to face the challenge of secular society, and leading their Christian lives within it. (Andrew Wingate, letter to the *Church Times*, 2 February 1990)

Many MSEs have a missionary perspective and describe their main purpose as

> to baptize the tiny bits of the world which each knows, into the Kingdom of God, where all shall grow together into full humanity, in proper relationship with one another and with God. (Michael Ranken, 'Ministry in Secular Employment and the Church's Mission', *Ordained Ministry in Secular Employment*, ACCM Occasional Paper no. 31, 1989)

The boundaries between Readers, NSMs and MSEs are very blurred, when seen in terms of Christian witness and mission, and the need for theological reflection. It may be that as *ministers* in employment NSMs and MSEs are 'marked' by their ordination, whereas Readers minister unobtrusively alongside other lay people as salt or yeast. Perhaps society – and the Church – needs both.

Different again are Local Ordained Ministers (LOMs), who are being encouraged in an increasing number of dioceses. In brief these are men (as far as I know there are no local ordained women deacons) whose ordination to the priesthood is an extension of the leadership which they have already been exercising within the local congregation. Some people view local ordained ministry as an expedient way of overcoming a shortage of priests, particularly in rural and inner-city parishes. Others claim that there are sound theological and sociological reasons for believing that a local ordained ministry is an appropriate response to the needs of Church and society. Theologically, there have always been men in the Church who have been recognized as spiritual leaders in their congregation, and who have been ordained to serve in their own limited locality. Sociologically, such leaders have been enabled to exercise a ministry within their communities in ways which priests of a different social class and culture could not hope to emulate. Their priesthood is a universal priesthood, but it is exercised within their own parish. LOMs differ from NSMs in that they are selected locally, and their training is locally based and appropriate to the functions they are likely to undertake. These may or may not include preaching.

As leaders in the local church, it is inevitable that some Readers are recruited as LOMs. Both exercise leadership in the congregation. Both are ministers of the Word, informally through study groups, pastoral visits and personal conversations, and Readers and some LOMs more formally in the liturgy through public preaching. LOMs also exercise a sacramental ministry. Readers work under the direction of the incumbent and may or may not be part of a team; LOMs work within a team of ordained and possibly lay ministers.

It is impossible to discuss Readers and other ministries without some reflection on the significance of ordination for clergy–Reader relationships.

> This concerns a differentiation between the priesthood of all believers, into which all Christians enter through baptism, and the sacramental priesthood which is the special calling of some particular members of the Church. Some Anglicans hold firmly to a belief that the Church of Christ is a Mystical Body, into which we are incorporated by baptism, and in which priests are sacramentally distinct from other members of it. Others hold, with the same strength of conviction, that clergy differ from laity only in function: they are simply set apart by the Church as teachers and pastors of the Christian community, equipping it for its ministry in the world. Again, some believe that priests depend for their call and for their authority solely upon God, while others maintain that the authority for priesthood comes not only from God, but derives also from the members of the Church in whose name such individuals are set apart. Still others would take an intermediate position. They believe both that ordained priests are fully part of the common royal priesthood of all the People of God, and that they also receive a call to exercise a particular and sacramental priesthood . . . ('The Common Statement', *All Are Called*, p. 5)

With such a range of understanding of ordination among clergy and lay people, including Readers themselves, some feel that the time has come for the Liturgical Commission (strengthened by the inclusion of at least an equal number of lay people – preferably 'unsynodical' – from inner cities and rural areas as well as suburbia) to rewrite the services for the ordination of bishops, priests and deacons to meet the needs of the Church *now*.

In the present Ordinal priestly functions expressed in traditional images reaffirm and possibly challenge the clergy, which is good. But as a Reader fortunate enough to live in a parish which has a curate, I find attendances at ordination services increasingly painful. We say we believe in shared ministry, but while the people are asked to declare their support for the new clergy in their ministry, no one asks the clergy to support the ministry of the people. The laity remain sheep, to be called to repentance and cared for, taught and admonished, fed and provided for, searched out and guided . . . all passive words. No wonder that the Church of England has a complaisant laity, or that Readers and other lay people feel their God-given talents are overlooked, even unwanted, in a clergy-dominated hierarchy. I do not wish in any way to diminish the ministry of the clergy – I owe much to some of them in my own pilgrimage, and I happen to think that they need caring for too. Rather I want to encourage them to explore the riches of genuine partnership, and to embody this in an ordination liturgy which gives value to all.

Whereas Readers and clergy together are ministers of the Word, only the clergy may administer the Sacraments, apart from dire emergency when any Christian may baptize someone who is in mortal danger. Some hold so firmly to the view that the ministries of Word and Sacrament are inseparable that they would turn all Readers into NSMs. At the other end of the spectrum others hold equally firmly that preaching is much more demanding than celebrating the Eucharist, and would permit Readers to celebrate forthwith. From the point of view of Church order either policy would simplify the structure, and avoid the practical difficulties which have arisen from a shortage of clergy in some areas. Unfortunately, life is not so simple. Quite apart from the inability of the Church to decide which option to choose, there are underlying theological and doctrinal issues which have to be teased out as part of the decision-making.

Two areas where the problems are felt most acutely by some, though not all, Readers, are concerned with baptism and the Eucharist. In many parishes Readers prepare families or candidates for baptism. Particularly where the people concerned have had little previous connection with the Church and are not known to the clergy, or where the Reader is virtually the pastor of the village, it would appear to make good pastoral sense for the Reader to baptize, and there are some clergy who would encourage this. Other occasions include emergencies where, through sudden illness, for example, a clergyperson is prevented from officiating, or interregnums, especially long interregnums, where again the Reader is the mainstay of pastoral care in the parish.

Holy Communion services are often a problem in rural areas where several parishes are grouped together under the leadership of one or two priests. On Sunday mornings the clergy spend their time driving from one church building to another, in a carefully arranged timetable which enables them to arrive in time to say the words of consecration at a service conducted by a Reader, and to rush off at the end to the next church, without ever meeting the members of their separate congregations.

Such arrangements, while praiseworthy in that they are designed to allow small congregations to celebrate the Eucharist every week, are plainly inadequate in terms of worship, Christian fellowship and pastoral care. One alternative is to permit the practice of Extended Communion, whereby the Reader, with the bishop's permission, distributes bread and wine which have been consecrated and reserved from a previous service. Though in practice this is less frustrating for both ministers and congregations, it too is inadequate, as it denies the worshipper the sense of being present at the heart of the service.

There are no easy solutions to these problems, pending the working out of an overall strategy by and for the Church. One can no longer pretend that the difficulties do not exist, and hope they will go away – they are likely to get worse. To encourage Readers to become NSMs or LOMs is to be in danger of creating 'mass-priests'. It also ignores the fact that women Readers cannot be priested and will be just as disabled as women deacons. It might be possible to permit the increasing use of Extended Communion, or to give specific permission to a very limited number of Readers to act as lay presidents of the Eucharist on stated occasions. Alternatively it might be more advisable to reduce the number of Communion services in each group of parishes, and to bring back Morning Prayer or an equivalent, in a positive endeavour to encourage more non-communicants to participate in worship. It is important to keep these matters in perspective. Readers are definitely not trying to acquire more power or prestige for themselves at the expense of the clergy. Probably fewer than half the Readers want or need their licences extended. In those places where there is proven pastoral need, Readers are already working with the good will and full support of the clergy and the people to whom they are ministering.

Readers or deacons?

The indecision of the Church of England concerning the diaconate has already been traced in Chapter 3. The debate continues, the most recent report, commissioned by the House of Bishops, being *Deacons in the Ministry of the Church* (General Synod no. 802, Church House Publishing, 1988). This report envisages permanent deacons being ordained to continue the ministry of Jesus, who came 'not to be served, but to serve' (Mark 10.45). Such deacons would serve both the community and the Church, and support the 'diaconal' or 'serving' ministry of all other Christians. It recommends 'that the Church of England make provision for, and encourage, men and women to serve in an ordained distinctive diaconate'.

Readers are commended for providing 'a highly valued ministry with a very definite accent on lay people trained to think theologically and able to communicate' (p. 66). The report, which implies that some Readers, though not all, would be ordained into this distinctive diaconate, has two significant drawbacks. First, it does not attempt to deal with the ambiguity of the Church's attitudes towards women deacons. It is plainly questionable to promote a diaconal ministry which must remain subordinate in character without, at the same time, considering how the Church may best use the ministry of its women. By implication the Church is denied the richness of a sacramental and complementary ministry of women and men together. Secondly, by advocating an ordained distinctive diaconate, the report belittles the vocation of *all lay people* to Christ's service by virtue of their baptism.

Does the Church want or need a permanent diaconate? The experience of some women deacons already suggests that, when it comes to *employing* them, the answer is in the negative. From another point of view, the Church has once again failed to come to terms with an educated laity. It has missed an opportunity to strengthen their vocation and commitment to 'every member ministry' in the world outside the Church, where God is already present among people, some of whom find the institutional Church a barrier to Christian faith and practice. *All Are Called* and *Called to be Adult Disciples* provide more space for authentic lay ministry, including Reader ministry, and more hope for 'Monday to Saturday night' Christians than any extension of a permanent, ordained, diaconal ministry.

'The Reader-shaped hole'

In a talk given in a personal capacity to Central Readers' Conference in March 1986, Canon Timothy Tyndall, then Chief Secretary of

ACCM, spoke of the 'supreme task of the Reader – the Reader-shaped hole'.

> The Reader has a place within the Liturgy of the Church: the Reader has knowledge and is trained to communicate. And the knowledge that is communicated both leads people out to serve and witness in the world, and also back into the heart of the Church, being built up by the Liturgy. (*The Reader*, August 1986, p. 81)

Such knowledge is born out of an understanding of Christian faith and life which draws upon the interplay of Scripture, tradition, reason and experience. Because of their experience in secular employment and in the life of the community, Readers are called to represent the world in the Church and the Church in the world. They embody within themselves unresolved tensions as they work out, by God's grace, the meaning of the Gospel. In practice this may mean being adventurous and taking risks which may not always be welcomed, understood or supported by the congregation at base. In the Church, Readers are called to resist being Church in an inward-looking sense; in society, they are called to resist being conformed to society's patterns of injustice and materialism.

There is another aspect of the Reader-shaped hole which Timothy Tyndall only hinted at. Among the people being led 'back into the heart of the Church' there will be those who are unfamiliar with the liturgy, and who, in an increasingly Eucharistic Church, will need to find a half-way house. One aspect of Reader ministry which needs to be given more prominence is the development of a lay spirituality. Some Readers have a deep spirituality which feeds on, and is fed by, the daily offices of the Church, the regular participation in Morning and Evening Prayer either alone or with others. Other Readers, however, are equally disciplined, but through different patterns of prayer and spirituality. There is scope here for Readers and other ministers, lay and ordained, to share together and to encourage one another, in order that they might better perceive the glory and the love of God, and help others to perceive it too. Such a ministry of spiritual direction, for those with appropriate gifts, needs greater encouragement than it is given at present, though there is at least one diocese where a small group of Readers meets regularly with an archdeacon to share their understanding and to learn together.

Travelling together

There is an untidiness about Church order which many people, ordained and lay, find difficult to live with. The role of the Reader is clear, to be a lay preacher and teacher within a pastoral context. Any attempt to describe how this role is worked out in the parishes leads at once into blurred areas where functions overlap with those of other ministers, lay and ordained. In many ways the Reader-shaped hole has to be created over and over again, balancing the individual gifts of Readers and their family, work and other commitments, with the particular staffing and needs of the parish at any given moment. All are likely to change, sometimes from one year to another.

A genuine partnership between clergy and Readers can only be expressed through a recognition and acceptance of differences. In the past too many Readers have aped the clergy, and too many clergy have tried to clericalize their Readers. Some Readers are unduly pressurized to become NSMs or LOMs – 'if only you could celebrate the Eucharist you would be so much more useful in the parish'. Yet there are Readers in every diocese who are grateful to their clergy who have given them opportunities to develop their strengths, encouraged them to discover and explore latent gifts, supported them in weakness, and above all shared with them the rough and smooth patches which make up the life of every parish.

Readers are now more positive about their lay status than they were ten years ago, when they seemed threatened by the development of new forms of lay and ordained ministries. They are finding opportunities for mission and service which are not always available to the clergy, and discovering God in the world outside the Church. For despite the labels we attach to people, God has ways of authenticating the ministries of all who are called, lay and ordained, within and outside the Church. Always the task is larger than we think, yet those who travel together in mutual trust find the Spirit beckoning ever forward into the new ways of thinking and new paths of service.

13: Links with the Anglican Communion

No survey of Reader ministry would be complete without mention of Readers in the world-wide Anglican Communion. This account of the life and work of Readers overseas cannot do justice to an unseen army of Readers. Their story requires another book!

Early days
The first references to lay ministers overseas occur in the Convocation of Canterbury in 1896 during a debate on lay evangelists, when it was reported that twenty members of the Wolverhampton Brotherhood, trained in Lichfield diocese, were serving overseas in the Bahamas, Ontario, Vancouver, Grahamstown and elsewhere. In 1904, a Convocation report, *Readers and Sub-Deacons* (no. 383), refers to Readers in Scotland, Ireland and the USA, in the 'Colonial Churches' of Canada, South Africa, Australia, New Zealand and the West Indies, and in the 'Missionary Churches' of India, China and Central and South Africa. *The Lay Readers' Official Directory 1906* (W. H. Lord, London), compiled and edited by the Rev. W. Henry Hunt, claimed to list 'all licensed, diocesan, parochial and stipendiary Readers in communion with the Church of England, at home and abroad, with full particulars of training, record of service, and the society (if any) to which he belongs'.

In South America, in British Guiana, there were 128 Readers, including twelve white, 70 negro or coloured, sixteen East Indians, four Chinese and four Aboriginal Indians. In this scattered colony there were 25 parishes with ten missions attached. Readers were licensed annually, their licences being 'best kept by incumbents'. Their sermons were read from books, Walsham How's *Plain Words* being especially recommended.

In the diocese of Sydney, Australia, one Reader exercised his ministry in 71 centres in 28 parishes in the course of a year. More than a hundred stipendiary Readers in 1910 were preparing for Holy Orders, 'a temporary and useful step . . . which would greatly relieve present necessities and strengthen the Church'.

In the diocese of Grafton, also in New South Wales, great care was taken in the selection of stipendiary Readers in 1912–13. Application forms covered education, including the level of languages, science and general subjects; trade, profession or secular employment; bankruptcy and debts. Licences could be withdrawn for serious impropriety or irregularity, or if Readers were unable 'whether from the insufficiency of the stipend or other reason' to keep out of debt, or for marrying without the express approval of the bishop. Stipendiary Readers normally resided with their vicar, and were expected to take a qualifying examination including Latin, New Testament Greek, Introduction to the Prayer Book, the History of England and a General Bible paper at the end of one year, as a preliminary to ordination training.

In Auckland, New Zealand, the bishop attempted to bring order out of the chaos of licensed and unlicensed Readers. Licences were to be delivered publicly 'for far-reaching educational effect'. The organization of Readers was decentralized. The key person in each area was an honorary librarian who also acted as local correspondent. By 1914 there were 270 Readers of whom 41 were Maoris. Communication was difficult with members in the back-blocks or remoter areas. The bishop encouraged Readers and affirmed the work they were doing: 'The joy of your work is the same as mine: we are fellow-workers with the Lord'.

The *Church of England Year Book* of 1914 included the following statistics of Readers in the Anglican Communion:

Provinces of Canterbury and York	4,060
Africa	1,733
Australia	1,641
New Zealand	1,001
India	895
Canada	859
West Indies	602
Far East	392
Pacific	49
Episcopal Church of America	2,955
	14,187

The Lay Reader also added 84 Readers in Scotland and four in Ireland, making a grand total of 14,275.

Glimpses of Reader ministry overseas

Readers in the Anglican Church overseas often bear all the marks of Readers in the Church of England, as is shown in the Bishop's Charge to Readers in the diocese of Colombo in 1928. Their work was to edify the faithful in the Christian community. Procedures of appointment had a familiar ring; the incumbent recommended, the bishop enquired; the Reader was licensed to work under the incumbent and had to be relicensed on a change of incumbent. He could preach only if his licence was endorsed, and then only from the lectern and never in the presence of clergy. He took no part in Holy Communion unless a priest was unfamiliar with the local language, in which case the Reader translated – from outside the communion rail. The Reader was expected to continue his studies. He was a person under authority as was his bishop. His privilege was to serve the Lord, and to live in conformity with his message.

In many dioceses Readers almost selected themselves, especially if they were expatriates. In the diocese of Egypt, which covered an immense area including Ethiopia, Aden, Eritrea and Cyrenaica, the regulations of 1947 set out the criteria for admission: vocation, personal character and standing, certain standards of general culture, physical fitness for public work especially leading worship, and general knowledge of the Bible and the Book of Common Prayer. Local people were recommended by the Native Christian Council before the bishop gave his decision. When licensed all served either as assistants to incumbents, or in small Christian communities where there were no priests, and where they helped to build and maintain Christian fellowship through leading prayer and worship. A few years later two Readers, one a Suez Canal pilot and the other working in the Anglo-Egyptian oil refinery, maintained the church in Suez which otherwise would have been closed.

Training was a constant concern, both before and after licensing. Some Churches did their best to maintain or adapt Church of England Readers' examinations, as did the diocese of Lagos with much correspondence to the CRB's training department. In 1969 Singapore asked for permission to translate the Board's new syllabus and study outlines into Chinese. In Uganda an indigenous scheme was evolved to suit local people and conditions, with a diocesan certificate awarded in three grades with corresponding responsibilities in the local church. Readers of the third grade were given charge of districts, and permitted to conduct Sunday services, preach, take baptismal and confirmation preparation and keep the accounts of their church. They were trained men of long experience; some of the better educated became clergy. Outstanding women teachers were given local responsibilities in the same way as Readers, preparing women and girls for baptism and confirmation.

Continuing education was a problem for many dioceses, especially where tiny Christian churches were scattered over wide areas with poor transport. Some, like Rangoon, attempted refresher courses by correspondence, supported by newsletters. Others, like British Guiana, brought Readers and catechists together in conference 'to keep before them the responsibility of their office and better equip them for their work'. In some areas there were monthly meetings, quarterly devotional services and annual retreats.

In the diocese of Huron, Canada, annual weekend conferences in the 1950s were concerned with the intellectual, devotional and practical training of Readers. Programmes included worship, lectures on biblical themes, sessions on sermon construction and voice production, and question and answer sessions on such topics as 'The Lay Reader and the Parish'. Parishes were encouraged to pay the conference expenses for their Readers.

It was easy enough to include in the objects of a Diocesan Readers' Association such phrases as that used by Sydney, Australia, 'to unite Readers for the purpose of strengthening their spiritual life, for the interchange of thought and experience, and for the promotion of sacred study'. Making it happen was quite another matter and often beyond available resources.

While as late as 1960 one bishop could claim 'We have no particular rules and regulations for Lay Readers in our diocese; we have 304 on the list', others were driven to action. In the 1950s a new bishop suspended all licences while the diocesan synod drew up new regulations to ensure that Readers were trained for various duties, thus discouraging 'local magnates and captains of industry' who had previously evaded their responsibilities. In another diocese the bishop established order by recognizing three categories of lay ministers: lay missionaries, who were educated and responsible in areas where there were no resident clergy; 'national' Readers, often working in similar situations, but in need of more 'feeding' with study and sermon material in the vernacular; and village catechists who, with little formal education, were key people in the local Christian community.

Occasionally the regulations remained impracticable, as in one very large diocese where a Reader was given special permission to administer the chalice at the request of the incumbent and church council on *each* occasion. Great sensitivity was sometimes shown, as when an African bishop acknowledged that 'diocesan rules for Readers are not in a state of fixity', but explained that different standards of education made regulations difficult to formulate without seeming to endorse apartheid.

There is no way of doing justice to the variety of work undertaken by Readers throughout the Anglican Communion. During World War II many Readers found themselves in strange circumstances, often beyond any formal connection with the Church, yet being the Church where they were. In 1942 a Reader who had been admitted in 1925 and licensed as a medical missionary in Upper Burma accompanied a party of convalescent officers and men of the retreating British army, and two missionaries en route for India. One Sunday night they camped in a tumbledown Kachin hut. Before them lay the hazardous crossing of the river Tarring, and a long difficult trek over the Naga Hills. Behind them were the advancing Japanese. The Reader led a short service, commending the party to God's loving care. 'From those grim hills where many perished, the faithful Lord brought all our party through to India and safety.'

Many Readers had virtually full care of Christian communities, often in very isolated locations. In Southern Rhodesia, for example, in parishes larger than Wales, Readers kept worship alive in remote farms, mines, homes, pubs and clubs or any available place, with the rector visiting at most once a month, but often at less frequent intervals. In other areas Readers travelled around. In Auckland the shortage of both priests and Readers meant that some communities had designated 'Church Sundays'. In Grafton, Readers travelled up to 6,000 miles each year.

Some expatriate Readers worked in missionary situations. A naval captain based in Singapore, for example, realized that language was more important than geography, and with other Readers helped to build up 'cottage churches' in homes, and extend a ministry to Asians. In Pittsburgh conditions were quite different and Readers were reminded never to read a sermon longer than fifteen minutes, and to conform to the custom of the congregation in matters of ritual. A cry from Trinidad might have been echoed in many dioceses: 'Many clergy ignore letters'!

Relations with CRB were maintained by correspondence, and sometimes by overseas visitors calling at the office. One wonders what Readers overseas felt on reading a letter from the office secretary in 1928:

> . . . We do feel that we should like the Colonial brethren to take some interest in what is going on at the Headquarters of the Readers Organization, and if they feel they cannot afford one

guinea per annum then half the amount would be better than nothing at all.

There was little overt criticism, but some of it was fair comment, as when the Ugandans complained in 1959 that *The Reader* gave too much space to notes, diocesan news, subscriptions and obituaries and not nearly enough to articles and items of overseas interest. On a more pleasing note the Readers of Auckland expressed warm appreciation of a 'whip round' from Guildford Readers towards training one of their number for ordination.

The Church's ministers need one another, and many bishops have shared their vision and offered Readers encouragement. One bishop always requested that a Reader should read the lessons when he visited, on the grounds that 'what is good enough for the bishop is good enough for the people'! A Bishop of Auckland, who knew of the difficulties of isolated ministry, wrote to his Readers:

> The Lay Reader needs at times to have a good heart and big stock of patience and power of endurance . . . Don't be too disappointed at a 'scanty congregation' for possibly there are one or two faithful sons in that congregation who are really hungering for spiritual food and drink which your service is able to supply.

There is appreciation of Reader ministry from a Bishop of San Joaquin, USA: 'The work, ministry and fellowship of Readers has enriched our Church life, and has been a constant reservoir of leadership for other phases of Church life'. And from a Bishop of Rangoon: 'The Lay Reader and catechist is not just a makeshift. He is part of the Church's fulfilment of our Lord's commission to all its members.'

Readers in the Anglican Communion today

This haphazard selection of 'snapshots' represents part of a family album of the Anglican scene; most members of the family are absent, and others are seen through the eyes of visiting friends. Starting in the Scottish Episcopal Church, in 1989 there were just over a hundred Readers of whom half serve in the united diocese of Glasgow and Galloway. The first woman Reader, a returned missionary, was licensed in 1974, and there are now fourteen. Three dioceses have under ten Readers.

The Episcopal Church in the USA has several forms of lay ministry. A confirmed adult communicant in good standing may serve as Lay Reader, Pastoral Leader, Lay Preacher, Lay Eucharistic Minister or Catechist if licensed by the bishop. Their respective duties are set out in Canon iii.3, *Of Licensed Lay Persons*. The Lay Reader 'is a person who regularly leads public worship' under the direction of the clergy in charge of the congregation, and it would appear that Readers' duties are much more limited than in the Church of England.

Two correspondents, in their very different ways, reflect how enterprising Readers may exercise a ministry which both enriches and is enriched. A recently retired doctor visited the Southern Sudan in his medical capacity, and having introduced himself to the local bishop, found himself invited to speak, often through an interpreter, on many occasions including a Readers' refresher course and an ordination retreat.

Two Readers from Birmingham diocese, having taken early retirement from teaching, spent six months in their link diocese of Malawi. They saw the work of the Church in different areas, and were able to use their expertise at diocesan headquarters. Following the death of her husband the wife made a second visit to Malawi, this time spending the first week at the annual Clergy Training Conference, and then visiting different parishes. An added bonus of working at the link in this way is that Malawians are encouraged to visit Birmingham and are welcomed into Christian homes. With other dioceses having links with overseas dioceses, and with more people retiring early, this is a form of service which Readers might consider more widely. It is no longer sufficient for bishops to meet together; lay people may sometimes break down barriers more easily. It is only by listening and sharing together that the people of God will discover the unity which already exists in Christ.

Readers in the Church of the Province of Southern Africa may have very varied experience of lay ministry, particularly if they move around the country. The diocese of Bloemfontein is almost the size of England, and divided into 50 parishes served by 46 priests. The diocese of Port Elizabeth also covers a vast area, but includes many large towns. In a city a Reader may do little more than lead the intercessions and serve as a Communion assistant. In a country parish there may be several scattered chapels where a Reader may be required to preach, teach, lead worship, make parochial visits, and take baptisms and funerals. Such a Reader must learn to be adaptable, as worship may take place in the open air, a mud hut or tin shed, or in a church building. The traditions of worship may vary from High to Low Church with all kinds of charismatic experience, 'a rich and rewarding tapestry'.

In a country of such wide contrasts, divisions, and expectations among different racial groups, Readers may find themselves sympathizing with genuine grievances of the underprivileged, and at the same time repelled by the political manipulation of situations and organizations to exploit people and gain political advantage. Service on the Bishop's Committee for Justice and Reconciliation may well be a challenge to both faith and temper.

A Reader and his wife working in Mogadishu in Somalia (*The Reader*, August 1988) stayed on to establish two projects, one to provide 'occupational therapy' for women psychiatric patients and the other to work among the street boys of the city. The projects were supported by Caritas Somalia, the charitable arm of the Roman Catholic Church, and TEAR Fund, with help from other sources, including the local Church, bridging the gap. The women's project was set up very quickly, that for the street boys took longer. In the meantime the Reader has been licensed to undertake pastoral responsibility, and some fifty people meet for worship in one of the Roman Catholic churches.

> At a typical service we will have Americans, Swedes, British, Germans, Dutch, Indians, Tanzanians, Ghanaians, Sierra Leonians, Koreans and so on, who may be Episcopalian but are as likely to be Lutherans, Methodists, Presbyterians, Baptists, Mennonites or whatever!

A teacher in Uganda became a Reader because the local clergy were accomplished preachers in Swahili and other local languages, but found English more difficult. Under the Amin regime the Reader's family were able to give hospitality to those in need, and on occasion acted as bodyguard for their Principal, just by being there. They later moved to Papua New Guinea, to a town with 30 churches, all different, and a primary school offering twelve different varieties of Christianity. When the Australian priest returned home the Reader was led to offer for ordination and was immediately accepted and ordained. His Reader's blue scarf is now proudly worn by a Papua New Guinea Reader.

The problem of reconciling different levels of thinking in the Church both at home and abroad is one of great concern to some Readers. One Reader worked as a liaison officer between the Protestant Churches' medical work in Kenya and Uganda and their respective Ministries of Health. Opportunities for preaching and pastoral ministry among medical workers of many nationalities forced him to try to work out a theology of the ministry of healing, which took account of both the scientific medical approach and forms of African healing in the context of their traditional religions. The spirit world of demons lurked not far beneath the surface, and preaching and ministry amongst the people had to take both worlds seriously.

On his return to this country to work at the headquarters of his missionary society he found it a constant struggle to link ministry in a London suburban parish with his experience abroad:

> The most poignant experience for me was after I had been sent to Uganda after the murder of Archbishop Janani Luwum . . . After sharing for some weeks with that sorrowing, persecuted and yet triumphant Church, I returned to my own parish and in the Service of Holy Communion there was no mention of Uganda . . . and its Church having lost their Archbishop, and no prayers for any other part of the world. I broke down in tears as I received Communion, remembering vividly my sermon in Namirembe Cathedral the previous Sunday, assuring the congregation of the prayers and support of Christians in Britain . . .

Much nearer home a correspondent now working in Germany has sent his Reader's 'job description'. He works in three episcopal jurisdictions. For the diocese of Europe, in the archdeaconry of Northern France, he takes services and preaches at St Catherine's church in Stuttgart. In the Catholic diocese of the Old Catholics in Germany he takes services in Nuremberg, and the Old Catholics have also 'lent' him to the Episcopalian Chaplaincy to the United States Armed Forces, also in Nuremberg. He works in two languages, uses four prayer books and attends three Annual General Meetings. With preaching, confirmation preparation and leading Bible study groups, one cannot but admire his energy and commitment, and envy his unique experience of the Church of Christ.

Two Readers have been privileged to take part in overseas Partnership in Mission consultations, one as a member of General Synod and the other as a staff member of a missionary society. The first, who visited the Church of the Province of Southern Africa, has written a vivid account in *The Reader* (February 1989), describing how she was able to meet people at opposite ends of the political and religious spectrums. The other visited the United Churches in Northern and Southern India, and found particular joy in speaking as a lay person and meeting lay people. Both are committed to the difficult task of representing the worldwide Church in their ministry as vividly as possible.

The Reader Missionary Studentship Association

Readers have corporately developed links with the Church overseas through their own charity, the Reader Missionary Studentship Association. In 1904, the Readers who attended the Summer Refresher Course at Keble were so impressed by the leadership of their Principal, Dr John Murray, and by his teaching and example that they wanted to show their gratitude in some tangible way. As Dr Murray was from 1903 to 1909 Warden of St Augustine's College, Canterbury, a missionary training college, the Readers decided to establish a studentship to enable Readers to be trained as priests for service on the 'mission field'. At that time there were no regular systems of grants available, either from educational sources or from the Church, and some of the students suffered real hardship. So the Reader Missionary Studentship Association, then called the Lay Reader Studentship Association, was founded.

The first student supported by the fund was ordained in 1910, and after that a steady flow of students served in more than fifty dioceses throughout the world. As grants became more widely available to Readers who felt called to the priesthood overseas, the Missionary Studentship Association sensibly looked for new ways of sponsoring Readers for ordination. While it has never forsaken its main aim, it has extended it to enable Readers overseas to train for the priesthood, either within their own countries or, more rarely, at colleges in this country.

The Association, now a registered charity within the Church of England, draws its funds mainly from Diocesan Readers' Boards and annual collections at Central Readers' Conference and at the Selwyn Refresher Course. There is also substantial support from some PCCs and individuals, and from the Harry Barnes Memorial Fund, set up to honour the Secretary of the Reader Missionary Studentship Association for many years. In 1988–89, £9,200 was given to 23 overseas Readers training in fourteen institutions, from Barbados through many parts of Africa to Papua New Guinea.

In human terms the benefits of the grants have been incalculable. Firm links have been established with theological and training colleges overseas, one of the most notable being Codrington College, Barbados, where students have been supported since the 1920s. The appointment of Drexel Gomez as Bishop of Barbados in 1971 meant that a former student, who studied first at Codrington and then at Durham, is in turn seeking the Association's support for his own students.

For those whose knowledge of the Anglican Communion is limited to the Church of England, the achievements of some Readers before starting their ordination training reflect remarkable faith, gifts and grace. A Sarawak Reader, for example, built a church with his own hands without waiting to tell the diocese. Another built up a Christian community in a previously non-Christian area which impressed his bishop as 'like the Early Church'. In Malawi a Reader was sent to a non-Christian district, and when his bishop arrived two years later he was amazed to find over eighty adult candidates prepared for confirmation, and two brick (not mud and wattle) churches. This gifted Reader, now ordained, speaks besides his own language, fluent English, Swahili, and the language of another area where previously work had been impossible.

These examples illustrate how worthwhile is the work of a charity like the Reader Missionary Studentship Association which encourages individuals with proven gifts in the service of God in so many different cultures. Incidentally, it will be interesting to see when, where and to whom the first grant will be given to a woman Reader to train for the ordained ministry as priest or deacon. There are always more applications for grants than the association can support. The place of the Reader Missionary Studentship Association as the Readers' own charity deserves continuing prayer and even greater financial support from all who value Reader ministry.

This account of some of the links between Readers in the Church of England and the Anglican Communion overseas offers signs for hope. Many bridges have been – and still are being – formed between Readers in a variety of cultures and with many different experiences of Christian faith. For most Readers, however, it remains true that our God is still too small.

14: The Ecumenical Scene

The prayer of Christ in St John's Gospel that 'all may be one' is a prayer echoed by many Christians today, but putting it into practice creates tensions for institutional Churches and their members. In this chapter I limit my comments to those 'mainstream' Churches in Britain where *authorized lay people* have a *preaching* ministry alongside ordained ministers. Besides the Church of England they are the Baptist, Methodist and United Reformed Churches, and the Presbyterian Church of Scotland.

Backward glances

During the nineteenth century no Church could keep pace with the increase in population. There were too few churches and too few ministers. While the Anglican umbrella sheltered Christians of many different standpoints, their practice of worship, though varied, was broadly centred on the Book of Common Prayer. The Nonconformists also had a recognizable identity. Their members had made a personal decision to accept God's offer of salvation; they believed in the Church as a gathered fellowship of men and women, consciously learning all they could of the will of God as seen in Jesus Christ, and working it out in the freedom of the Holy Spirit. They believed in the priesthood of all believers, ordained and lay, women and men, and in their calling to live by, and witness to, the gospel.

Within this spectrum of common beliefs, each denomination reflected its particular nuances of Church life which influenced the way in which their lay ministries developed. The Methodists developed a highly centralized organisation through their annual Conference. Local Preachers remained in their own neighbourhood or circuit. Methodist ministers were all drawn from the ranks of Local Preachers, and after further training were ordained to an *itinerant* ministry, that is, they were moved by Conference from church to church at more or less regular intervals.

The United Reformed Church was formed in 1972 by the coming together of most of the constituent churches of the Congregational

Union of England and Wales and the Presbyterian Church of England. The much smaller Churches of Christ joined a few years later. From the mid-nineteenth century every Congregational church expected to have its own ordained minister, while *lay* preachers were able to supply pulpits and teach and preach in mission rooms. Thus in the United Reformed Church the tradition has been for the minister to be static in the larger churches, and for lay preachers to move around the smaller churches in local areas.

Baptists, like the Congregationalists and their ancestors, the Independents of the late sixteenth and seventeenth centuries, have a long tradition of lay preachers and pastors serving local churches. The large town churches were eventually served by ordained ministers. But elsewhere a church might be able to call either a minister setting out on his career, one looking towards retirement, or, more recently, a part-time minister in secular employment. Where churches exist in rural areas or when new churches are planted, they are generally served by lay preachers.

The Church of Scotland resembles the Church of England in that both are national Churches serving the whole community whereas the Free Churches minister to 'gathered' congregations. In the Church of Scotland a wide variety of ministries has evolved over many years: ordained ministers, licensed ministers, elders (also ordained), deacons, home missionaries, readers, and more recently, auxiliary ministers. In the Church of Scotland and the Church of England, Readers have had both a shorter history and a less important role than lay preachers in the Free Churches. Without local and lay preachers some Baptist, Methodist and United Reformed fellowships would not have survived.

New perspectives

Changes in Church and society have challenged all the Churches to reappraise their theology of ministry in the light of their calling to proclaim the gospel and to work for the coming of the Kingdom of God. In urban areas, church buildings are often in the wrong places, away from where most people live, while in rural areas the policy has often been one of withdrawal. Apart from some Baptist churches, there has been a steady decline of church membership and a failure to recruit and maintain an adequate number of ordained stipendiary ministers. The prevailing materialist outlook in society, together with the pressures of inflation, have led to insufficient funding for both ministry and the work of all Churches. Each denomination has been forced independently to take stock and to develop policies and priorities for the future. Consultations in each Church have started at different times and reached different stages, yet three strands common to all may be distinguished: *working out a theology of ministry, extending ordained ministry* and *reappraising lay ministry.*

In many areas Churches are working more closely together and there has been a steady increase in the number of Local Ecumenical Projects. These are officially designated schemes where local Churches of more than one denomination, with the agreement of their appropriate governing bodies, covenant to work together and to share their resources.

The Church of Scotland's Panel on Doctrine Report to the General Assembly in 1989 holds that our understanding of ministry must be grounded in the ministry of Christ, the Son of God, who is sent into the world in the power of the Holy Spirit. The mission of the Son is to reconcile the work to God and enable human beings to share in the life of fellowship, united with Christ and caught up into the eternal fellowship of the Godhead. The Christian community is a sign and anticipation of God's Kingdom. It is a community of the redeemed in which divisions of sex, class and race are overcome, and which is called to witness through proclamation and service. This ministry, derived from, and part of, Christ's ministry, is understood as a calling of the *whole* Christian community rather than of individuals within it. Yet each individual has a unique part to play in the Church's ministry by virtue of being baptized into the Body of Christ. This ministry of the baptized, of the *laos*, the whole people of God, is directed primarily towards the mission of Christ in the world and in the local community, in all aspects of life.

Such a calling of the whole people of God presupposes that some men and women are called to exercise leadership to enable all their members to live in the service of Christ. All Churches are seeking ways of expressing corporate leadership through ordained and lay ministries working together. In practice, most are still at the stage where the ordained minister, whether man or woman, is regarded as ultimately responsible for the good ordering of worship; for encouraging the building-up of a community of faith and the bearing of one another's burdens; and for working out the faith in the community. Thus there is often a yawning gap between the way that the Churches understand ministry and the way they exercise it in practice.

The failure of the Churches to provide adequately for a traditional form of ordained ministry may be regarded by future ecclesiastical historians as a blessing, for it has compelled the Churches to think more deeply about their whole ministry. Ordained ministers are now found in a wider variety of callings, including ministries in industry, health, education and the caring professions. Some ordained ministers are no longer dependent on Church funding, but continue in secular employment and exercise their ministry at work and in the local church. Happily, it is no longer possible to draw a firm boundary between ordained ministers and the rest of God's people.

While it is true that every Christian is called to serve God, the great majority exercise this genuine lay ministry among those with little or no understanding of, or allegiance to, Jesus Christ. Such Christians need to be equipped for this task and to be supported in it. This in itself calls for a wider range of gifts, skills and expertise than any one person, ordained or lay, could possibly offer. This need for a corporate ministry of ordained and lay together makes possible a greater diversity and richness of ministry which may well be one of God's gifts to our generation. Unfortunately it has sometimes been marred in the past by unseemly rivalry, threatened feelings, and a lack of understanding and generosity of spirit. Recognized lay ministers have a special calling to interpret the Church to the world and the world to the Church because their discipleship is exercised in both. They embody in their own persons the tensions of both in a way not open to the ordained stipendiary minister.

If lay preachers exercise this complementary role to the ordained minister, they no longer deserve to be regarded as stop-gap ministers and substitutes for the 'real' minister. This will involve changes in perspectives and expectations on the part of congregations, of many ministers and of lay preachers themselves.

> There have been plenty who have given lay preaching a bad name, by playing no part of any kind in their own congregation, having only a nominal settled life in a worshipping group, who have gypsied about, wandering minstrels of the gospel . . . their arrogance increased in inverse proportion to their gospel. (The Rev. A. G. Burnham, 'Lay Preaching, an Outdated Concept', an address given to a meeting of Lay Preachers' Commissioners, United Reformed Church, 1988)

At their worst there have been lay preachers in all Churches who have tarnished the image of the lay minister. At their best their preaching has a genuine prophetic edge, as the Spirit illumines their understanding of Scripture and tradition in the light of their engagement with the contemporary world. This latter understanding is becoming part of the thinking of all those concerned with the development of lay ministry, though it will take some time to work its way into the life of all the Churches.

From lay preachers we need preaching which is rooted in real relationships with the worshipping congregation . . . which uses the experience of the everyday to interpret and announce the Word of God to feed our hungry people. (United Reformed Church).

Methodism must have local preachers because it needs the Gospel spoken out of the context of the secular world; it must hear the expression of Christian faith that has been tested and deepened . . . in those situations that the people in the pews spend their working lives. In this way local preachers complement ministers in the pulpit ministry to the Methodist people.

Lay preachers, because their discipleship is lived out on the frontiers of the Church's engagement with the world, should be able also to interpret the needs of the world into the Church, thus enabling, in turn, the Church to ensure that its concerns, the issues with which it grapples, the way in which God's people are equipped, all remain relevant to its task of mission. (Baptist)

If lay preachers are to live up to their calling, then it is essential that the Churches equip them to think about the nature of true Christian discipleship within a secular society. This presupposes rigorous policies of selection and training, involving both the local congregation and the wider Church. Methodists, for example, are authorized to assist a fully accredited preacher in the conduct of services within the circuit for a period of three months 'on note', before proceeding to a period of two to three years 'on trial'.

There is now more emphasis on the appropriateness of training for *lay* ministry, rather than seeing it as a watering down of the training given to the ordained. Current adult education methods are being used more widely and include the development of communication and pastoral skills. The integration of practical work with the whole of training is common. Candidates are assigned to local tutors who are themselves often required to undergo training for their tutorial task. It is hoped that if people enjoy their training they will want to continue their learning after initial accreditation, grow in their understanding of Christian faith and life, and enable the people of God to live out their discipleship in a rapidly changing and complex society.

Readers in Local Ecumenical Projects
Many Readers find themselves participating in Local Ecumenical Projects *after* admission, but the Churches in and around Swindon

have organized a scheme of *joint training* involving Anglican, Methodist, Baptist and United Reformed Church participants. The proposal originated in an ecumenical day conference in Bristol in 1980. During the following nine years four groups have been organized, involving some 30 candidates. The course was based in Swindon where there are seven Local Ecumenical Projects, all but one including Anglicans.

There were four main reasons for promoting joint training: it provided opportunities for trainees to learn from one another; it underlined the value of Readers and lay preachers in their own right, and not as substitutes for ordained ministers; it was more economical in demands on tutors and on travelling (previously Readers had attended courses in Bristol, 40 miles away); it enabled a variety of tutors from the different denominations to contribute. Provisional selection and final accreditation or approval continued on denominational lines. When further tuition on denominational teaching was required it was provided for *all* the participants, enabling them to learn about one another's traditions. Most of the trainees, including Anglicans, expressed their appreciation of the enrichment which came through the ecumenical fellowship of studying together. In the ebb and flow which seems to mark ecumenical life the scheme has not been so well supported recently, perhaps because of the rethinking of training among Anglicans and others, but I am assured that the commitment to joint training remains and the intention is to go forward.

In some areas Anglican Readers enjoy very good relations with their counterparts in other Churches, particularly with Methodist Local Preachers, having joint deanery–circuit meetings for study and fellowship. Where these take place, some Readers are regularly included on the 'plan' of quarterly services in the circuit. It is not so common, however, for Local Preachers to be included on Anglican rotas. There is scope for much more interchange than at present takes place, both in churches and in the whole field of continuing education and in-service training.

A few Readers have trained under more than one scheme. One Reader decided after licensing to continue her learning by undertaking the joint Baptist, Methodist and United Reformed Church Course, *Exploring the Faith*. In an area where ecumenical relationships were already friendly the local United Reformed Church minister was appointed her tutor, and two years and seventeen units of study later she was also awarded her United Reformed Church lay preacher's certificate. This dual training has enriched her understanding of both traditions, broadened her preaching and enlivened youth parades and informal worship services. As she trains for stipendiary ministry in the Church of England, she is undergirded with 'ecumenical prayer and the benefit from excellent ecumenical foundations'.

Not all ecumenical experiences are positive. Frustration is an integral part of life in many an ecumenical parish, especially for those Readers who become involved in its organization. Some have discovered, with lay leaders of other participating Churches, that however bright their vision of unity and however much energy they put into moving forward, clergy have their own ways of preventing action. This is particularly true where ministerial appointments are made without giving priority to the needs of the ecumenical project. It can be disastrous when the five principal clergy change within three years! A lay chairperson, even a Reader or Local Preacher, has a difficult task made almost impossible by being left out of staff discussions. And congregations lose out too, when quarterly pulpit exchanges involve ordained ministers only, and never include Readers or local and lay preachers, however highly qualified and experienced.

The best ecumenical work is achieved where it is *really needed*, rather than being an optional extra for churches which are fully staffed, have their own buildings and sufficient funding to get by. One Local Ecumenical Project is situated in an Urban Priority Area in an East London borough, said to be the second most socially deprived in the whole country. The Roman Catholics are full participants (the building includes a permanent statue of Our Lady, with votive candles) with Methodists, Baptists, United Reformed Church members and others probably outnumbering Anglicans. Traditional Anglican (Alternative Service Book) services are not held every Sunday; Free Church patterns are more usual. Preaching is demanding, for one has to begin by learning where other Christians are. Overall there is a keen enthusiasm to make the sharing work. While it would be wasteful to duplicate buildings and other resources – including people – the need to succeed runs deeper. Amid the divisions within society as a whole and within the local community, this ecumenical church is a sign of Christian unity and caring.

The Reader attached to this church not only lives in the parish, he is also politically active, as the sole member of the opposition on his local council, living in the ward which he represents. In this capacity he deals with the homeless and disabled and those with poll tax arrears. 'Compassion is easy: trying to allocate resources between conflicting priorities takes a little more care.' So part of his commitment is working out a strategy for economic regeneration. This Reader believes that if we take the Incarnation seriously we cannot shut ourselves away from public affairs, and that if we really believe God is alive and reigning, we must work for increasing order and justice. The ecumenical parish is for him the base for his ministry and for sharing his insight into the working out of the Kingdom of God.

Sometimes Readers spend time overseas as part of their secular employment. In some locations they are drawn into Christian fellowships which are both ecumenical and international. As an example I have drawn on the experience of a Reader in a small congregation in Jakarta a few years ago. The Australian incumbent was an evangelical, one Reader was an Anglo-Catholic, the other 'central' – and also churchwarden; the treasurer was an American Baptist, the organist a Roman Catholic Chinese, and for a period they were joined by a distinguished Swiss leprosy surgeon who had taken Indian nationality and was also a priest of the Church of South India. Such a rich diversity of Christians living in 'joyful fellowship' adds new dimensions to the experience of all participants, and to their understanding of the Church.

In 1989 the Church of England took a further step forward in ecumenical relations with the approval of Canons B43 and B44. These Canons concern the role of ministers in Local Ecumenical Projects, and more widely in relationships with other Churches. They authorize Readers to minister in churches of other denominations to the extent that they are licensed to minister in their own parishes. These Canons encourage the practical expression of ecumenical activities on a wider front than sponsored Local Ecumenical Projects. In some areas Readers, through their parishes and deaneries, may well begin to take initiatives or to respond to those taken by other Churches, to work more closely together, and to express their growing co-operation in services of worship as well as in action.

Joint Readers' and Preachers' Conferences

For many years Methodist Local Preachers have held an annual weekend conference at Selly Oak, Birmingham. At the time of the Anglican–Methodist Conversations an invitation was issued to Readers to join them. Since then the invitation has been further extended to include lay preachers of the Baptist, Congregational Federation and United Reformed Churches. As far as I am aware the conference has no formal standing in any of the Churches. It is organized by a committee of the officers concerned with Readers and local and lay preachers in their respective Churches, with representatives of the lay ministers themselves. Among the fifty or so attending are a small core who participate every year, and some who are attracted by the conference theme. In recent years themes have included Christian Ethics and Society Today, Faith in the City, Worship, Spirituality, Resurrection Then and Now, and Emerging Lay Ministries – Has the Preacher a Place?

I believe the Joint Readers' and Preachers' Conference works as yeast in the denominations. In relation to the total numbers of Readers and Preachers, only a few are able to participate, but through worship, often part familiar and part unfamiliar, participants are drawn closer to God and to one another. In exploring the theme they are privileged to listen to leaders, ordained and lay, of their own or other Churches, and are challenged in their thinking. As they work at the theme in small groups they share their insights into the richness and diversity of both Church and society, and discover that what works well in one context may be inappropriate in others. And in the social life which forms part of any conference there is an informal building-up of the Body of Christ which refreshes and renews those present. So Readers and Preachers return home, and the conference experience is taken into the life of the Church, often in ways which remain unrecognized – like yeast.

I have looked at the ecumenical scene through spectacles which were not able to focus on the bigger stages of the British and World Councils of Churches. Readers have been fortunate in having among their number people like Jean Mayland, who has been privileged to serve both the BCC and the WCC with distinction, and who is now President of the Ecumenical Forum of European Christian Women. This wider experience informs their preaching and their commitment to Church life wherever they are. On the other hand it may also deepen their despair and frustration at the general lack of vision, imagination and concern among Readers as among many Church members. These Readers have responded to a privileged but difficult calling. They need more support, including prayerful support, than they often receive. Though by comparison with the body of Readers they are few in number, they act on behalf of all.

The Christian Church cannot rest until it has recovered that unity which already exists in Jesus Christ, and to which he calls all his followers, whatever labels they attach to themselves and despite all their differences. Some Readers maintain that this entails working within ecclesiastical institutions, changing rules as opportunities arise, but holding on to truth as it is perceived and understood within the tradition. Other Readers have a stronger perception of the development of the tradition in the light of truth as it is revealed in the interplay of Scripture, tradition, reason and experience. There is no doubt that Christian divisions greatly dishonour God and make it more difficult for God's people outside the Church to recognize the God of love in the world around them. As authorized lay ministers, Readers are called to work for unity as a sign and anticipation of the Kingdom of God. The opportunities exist. What more might Readers do, both individually and corporately, to make real within a divided, and therefore disabled, Church, that unity which already exists in Christ and which offers healing to a troubled world?

15: Celebration and Change

125 years of Reader ministry

The Church of England has good cause for praising and thanking God for 125 years of Reader ministry. From very uncertain beginnings in 1866 when the office of Reader was revived in the Church of England, the Reader movement has grown into a body of over 8,000 men and women exercising a voluntary, lay ministry which is nationally accredited, episcopally licensed and governed by Canon. Readers are recognized and accepted by clergy and laity alike in every diocese in the Church of England, and in most parts of the Anglican Communion.

Take away the present Readers and in many dioceses it would be impossible to maintain a Sunday service in every parish every week. The Church's ministry would be impoverished and impaired, not only on Sundays but during the week as well. Much work would be left undone, and a much heavier load would be placed on the clergy especially, as well as on other lay people, in pastoral care, leading house-groups and a host of other tasks which help to build up the people of God. In the wider mission of the Church, too, the representative role of the Reader would be lacking. Many who are untouched by the institutional Church have cause to be thankful for the faith and Christian insight which Readers have shared with them in their homes and at work. Readers, by their lay status, are particularly called to enable the people of God to work for the Kingdom of God, wherever God is to be found in creation.

At first Readers were only permitted to do what any member of the laity might do in consecrated buildings. Progress toward the present wide-ranging ministry of Readers has been slow, erratic and piecemeal. It has depended partly on the character and ability of Readers themselves, and partly on the encouragement of the clergy and on the more muted support of congregations. When opportunities for service occurred, Readers were moved by the Spirit to respond. Sometimes they ignored the niceties of ecclesiastical order to meet obvious pastoral needs, often with the good will of clergy unable to cope with all the demands of over-large urban or widely scattered rural parishes.

While Readers have given their services freely to the Church, it has not been without cost, in terms of soul-searching, time, energy and effort, family life, and the stipendiary Readers' great financial sacrifice. Despite the achievements, Reader ministry has had – and still has – its darker side. Not all Readers were capable of undertaking the tasks assigned to them. Some were inadequately prepared, and others, after becoming Readers, have tried to preach with closed minds, insensitive to the needs of their congregations. Too many clung to office, nationally and in the dioceses, when they should have handed over to a younger generation. But the overall picture remains one of a lay ministry which has for 125 years gradually gained the respect and the confidence of the Church.

In a wider perspective much progress has also been made towards integrating Reader ministry within the whole ministry of the Church. From the early diocesan Reader associations of the 1880s and the first steps towards a national organization with the Annual Conference on Readers' Work, Readers have attempted to extend their usefulness in the service of the Church. At first such organization was highly desirable for mutual encouragement, training and fellowship, but Readers did go through a stage when it seemed as if centrally their aims were to establish and cling to some kind of independence under the Church's umbrella. On its part the national Church, through Convocations and Church Assembly, was grudging in its recognition of Readers, and dilatory in extending their duties despite proven pastoral need. While paying lip-service to the priesthood of all believers, it discouraged it when it showed signs of emerging in the lay ministry of Readers. As the plight of stipendiary Readers became more widely known, the Church virtually abandoned all responsibility until very late in the day.

In the last two or three decades, however, relationships have completely changed. With the advent of General Synod in 1970, Readers became for the first time integrated within the government of the Church, while Central Readers' Conference retained responsibility for its own internal affairs. Thus Readers are open to new developments at the centre and, at the same time, are able to share their particular expertise from the perspective of accredited lay ministers in the committees of the Church. Many Readers look forward to the day when General Synod and Central Readers' Conference together will be able to finance a full-time Reader Executive Officer or the 'Organizing Secretary' first envisaged by Dr John Murray some seventy years ago.

Readers, along with Church Army Evangelists, are a sign of the whole ministry of the Church, and of men and women ministering together in equal partnership. It is a sign which the Church of England, well behind certain other provinces of the Anglican Communion, has yet to recognize in the fullness of ordained ministry. In the parishes the quiet presence of women Readers, whose numbers are steadily increasing, together with the higher profile of women deacons, is giving more people opportunities of experiencing women's ministry and paving the way for the eventual ordination of those women whom God is calling to the priesthood.

Celebrations are like signposts. They mark the road which has already been travelled and they point the way ahead. Although Readers are moving forward in the same direction, they are so diverse a company, with such riches in gifts, skills and life experience among them, that they are certain to journey along interweaving paths. An increasing number are likely to find themselves living with the paradoxes and ambiguities of faith as they turn the Church's vision outward, and bear witness to the love of God whose creative and redemptive grace is made known in Jesus Christ, and in the Spirit working in the lives of his followers.

This development of a theology implicit in lay experience imposes a task on Readers where all are called upon, individually and corporately, to act, reflect, interpret, and pray, as part of their willing obedience and commitment to God. Three recent reports, *Selection for Reader Ministry*, *The Training of Readers* (ACCM Occasional Paper no. 32), and *Bishops' Regulations*, will enable the ministry of Readers to become even more effective in future.

Selection for Reader Ministry: A report on criteria and good practice
The selection of candidates for Reader ministry is the responsibility of the dioceses, usually acting through the Warden of Readers in consultation with the bishop. Selection methods vary from a single interview with the Warden to sophisticated pre-vocational courses and very formal and searching selection procedures. Following discussions of the 1986 Wardens' report, a working party was set up 'to prepare and provide criteria for selection and a guide to good practice for use by the dioceses'; it reported in January 1990.

Instead of summarizing the report, I outline the paths of three would-be Readers, Tom, Ann and Jim, through the selection process. Ann is already a member of the diocesan Faith and Ministry Course, a one-year course available at several centres and open to all who want to explore together their Christian faith and ministry. Tom has been an active member of his congregation for many years, but Jim is younger and full of enthusiasm, having converted to Christianity about a year ago. They have all been recommended for consideration for Reader training (admission is the responsibility of the Bishop and Warden) by their incumbents and PCCs. The Warden has visited Jim and Tom informally at home, but as Ann lives at the other end of the diocese she has been visited by the Deputy Warden. As soon as their names were forwarded the Warden sent them publicity leaflets relating to Reader and other forms of ministry, lay and ordained. The Warden also sent the diocesan leaflet outlining the selection procedure, and inviting them to come for interview, with full details of the date, time and place, together with a map. The leaflet also explained when and how they would be notified of the outcome.

Mary, a Reader, is a tutor and one of the panel of selectors, together with other men and women, ordained and lay. All the selectors have been given notes to guide them on the procedure, the criteria for selection and the diocesan scheme for Reader training. A week before the interviews they were sent copies of the candidates' forms and references. Mary and two others interview Tom and Jim, but Ann is interviewed by a different panel meeting in her archdeaconry. Both panels assembled to plan the interviews before the candidates arrived. As a guide they used the six criteria set out in the report: vocation, faith, spirituality, personality and character, relationships, and quality of mind. They point to avenues for the selectors to explore in the light of candidates' own gifts, diverse opportunities for Reader ministry and local circumstances.

The selectors discovered that Tom was a person of deep faith and already recognized as a leader in his parish. Though he was diffident about the prospect of preaching, his vicar was confident that, with training, he had the makings of a good preacher. The panel was impressed with Jim's enthusiasm and his rapid growth in the faith, but felt he still had a lot to learn about the basics of Christian belief and practice. Ann's panel discovered that she was already doing a lot of pastoral visiting which was leading her towards sharing her faith in a more public way.

In the discussions which followed the interviews, it was agreed that Ann and Tom should go forward for Reader training. The panel was divided about Jim. On balance, they recommended that he should apply for a place on the diocesan Faith and Ministry Course and re-apply for Reader training next year. All the candidates and their incumbents were notified of the decisions within a week. The Warden also telephoned Jim and his incumbent, and invited Jim to come and see him, in order to give him some encouragement. Written reports on each of the accepted candidates identified some of their strengths and weaknesses. These diagnostic reports, to be destroyed on completion of training, were sent to the Deputy Warden who supervises Reader training. Mary and the other interviewers have been paid all their travelling and other expenses by the Diocesan Readers' Board. Tom's and Jim's expenses were paid by their PCCs, but Ann was left to pay her own.

This important report on the selection of Readers attempts for the first time to draw up nationally agreed criteria for selection for Reader ministry, supported by good practice, but the onus remains with the dioceses. Central Readers' Conference also has a role to play, ensuring that there is a supply of lively and attractive publicity material (the Methodists seem to be much better at this!), together with standard application forms, letters and notes to ease selection procedures. Those concerned with selection for Reader ministry have for the first time been given a clear and detailed map. As all walkers know, sometimes the tracks are not so clear on the ground and the least likely acquaintances turn out to be the best companions. But that is no excuse for throwing the map away!

The Training of Readers: the report of the working party of the Committee for Theological Education

This substantial 80-page report (ACCM Occasional Paper no. 32, November 1989) could well mark the beginning of a new era in Reader training. It owes its origin to two events in 1986, the publication of the Wardens' report on *The Ministry and Training of Readers*, and the transfer of responsibility for the training of Readers from Central Readers' Conference to ACCM's Committee for Theological Education. This significant step gave public recognition to Reader ministry as an integral part of the whole ministry of the Church. At present only a quarter of those admitted annually to Reader ministry have completed the General Readers' Certificate, the rest having been trained under a variety of diocesan schemes. While respecting the academic rigour in training that has been the major achievement in recent years, the new scheme sets training in a wider context. The new proposals depend on a working partnership between the centre, through ACCM's Committee for Theological Education, and the dioceses working individually but co-operating in regional groupings.

The report stresses the need to take serious account of the setting, culture and ethnic mix of the parish and neighbourhood of potential Readers, as well as the gifts and skills individuals bring with them as starting points for their training. Initial Reader training aims to prepare participants for accredited ministry by helping them to grow in their love and response to God through prayer, worship and service; to continue to develop their understanding of the Christian faith and their capacity to communicate and proclaim it; and to develop appropriate skills for Reader ministry.

The criteria, which provide a working guide for the development, assessment and review of diocesan schemes, are set out under four headings: The Appropriateness of the Training on Offer; Theological Content; Educational Methods; Assessment during Training and Final Assessment.

The key figures, as far as Readers in training are concerned, are the local tutors. Tutors with a good theological background and an understanding of, and commitment to, Reader ministry will additionally need to be familiar with a wide range of learning methods now used in adult education. The key person in the scheme is the honorary National Moderator, who is the link between the centre and the dioceses. Already under his encouragement and guidance the new scheme is beginning to take shape.

This report also envisages the continuing education of Readers after admission. Newly licensed Readers are encouraged to add breadth or depth to their initial learning by participating in a variety of courses provided by the Church or other agencies. New proposals for the Archbishops' Diploma offer an opportunity to explore in depth some aspects of the Christian faith and life. Candidates will have a choice to pursue a theme in depth in one of five areas: the relationship between theological and/or biblical study and the contemporary world; the biblical or Christian traditions; the relationship between the Christian faith and the candidate's own professional or community interests; inter-faith dialogue and understanding; and the communication of the faith through the arts or new technology. The work, which may include other related disciplines, will be supervised throughout, and moderated in two stages. The study, which is estimated to take from two to four years depending on the candidate's circumstances, may be presented in the form of a project, a dissertation, an original work in the creative arts, or an original use of the media, with an annexed theological explication if appropriate.

It is expected that this imaginative scheme for the Archbishops' Diploma for Readers will encourage not only more Diploma candidates, but also the development of similar forms of continuing education at different levels for Readers and other lay ministers. While continuing education is desirable for all Readers, it must be open to the needs of Church and world, and enable individual Readers to discover and develop their latent gifts.

The proposals in *The Training of Readers* report represent a giant leap forward. For the first time ever, the Church is awarding a Church of England Reader's Certificate to all Readers who complete training. Dioceses will be working in closer partnership with the centre, and Reader training is now spelt out in educational as well as theological terms.

In my experience, when people enjoy their training (and that includes the manner as well as the content) they come back and ask for more. Not necessarily more of the same, but more to satisfy mind and spirit and to increase their skills in serving others. As a member of the Working Party, it is my hope that the new plans for Reader training will encourage the development of more imaginative and creative forms of lay and clergy education too.

Bishops' Regulations

Reader ministry is formally integrated with the life of the Church by means of Canon and by Bishops' Regulations, that is, rules which are approved from time to time by the House of Bishops as part of the ' episcopal oversight of ministry. A third Working Group also reported in 1990, recommending that the Regulations, which have not been updated since 1969, should be revised to take account of the current nature of Reader ministry.

The report recommends that licences should be renewed every three years, and that at the age of 70 Readers should return their licences and, if they wish to continue in active ministry, apply for permission to officiate. Other recommendations concern representation on PCCs, Readers and interregnums, annual reports and the pastoral discipline of Readers. The principal recommendation, however, suggests that a 'Reader and Baptism' working party should be set up through ACCM, with wide representation, 'to consider and report on the current and future role of Readers in relation to Baptism . . . in the light of the profound theological and pastoral issues involved, including aspects of the theology of Ministry and the Sacraments'.

While the nature of regulations is to bring a semblance of order where variety of practice abounds, it is likely that pastoral awareness, and the idiosyncrasies of both bishops and Readers, will always inhibit uniformity of interpretation throughout the Church of England. These new proposals provide acceptable guidelines for good practice, and will in due course be considered by the House of Bishops. In the meantime Readers will continue their ministry, and a few bishops will not yet allow them to perform all the duties permitted by Canon.

Bold to preach

Readers stand in the tradition of the apostles, who again and again are depicted in the Acts of the Apostles as 'preaching with all boldness'. When the office of Reader was revived in 1866, few people could have envisaged the development of a lay ministry with a liturgical role which included regular preaching from the pulpit in church. At the present time it is this call to preach which characterizes Reader ministry, and distinguishes Readers from other authorized lay ministers.

Even after training in theology and in the skills of communication, most Readers, and not only the newly licensed, are likely to describe feelings of 'trepidation' rather than 'boldness' before preaching. At the same time they are aware, in the words of the second Collect for Pentecost, of being sent out 'in the power of the same Spirit to witness to your truth and to draw all peoples to the fire of your love'. This task demands that Readers struggle with the tensions of relating their faith to the whole of life, and the whole of life to their faith. They can only do this by reflecting prayerfully in the light of Scripture, tradition, reason and experience, in order to discern and proclaim the love of God at work in the world.

In my mind's eye I have a vision of future Readers utterly committed to preaching, teaching and serving God in the world as *lay* people. But with a difference! Let me ask some hard questions. Will Readers be found reinforcing society's values, or attempting to discern and work out Christian values at work and in the community? Conforming to society's norms in government, the city, commerce and industry, or co-operating with others, including non-Christians, to shape society's future? Will they seek to protect Christian privileges, or join the struggle for justice and human rights?

In the Church, are Readers as a body too conformist, too predictable, and too often deservedly overlooked? What is their view of authority? Does their ready acceptance of authority in the Church encourage a dependence which is a little too convenient for everyone? Do they not need to struggle at a deeper level with themselves, their faith and authority, if they are to express at all adequately their understanding of human beings made in the image of God and becoming new persons in Christ? Will they avoid conflict at all costs, or will they live out something of the redemptive grace of God in centres of reconciliation? Are Readers to look for comfort and security, or will they be found in the thick of the action, at risk, vulnerable and involved in the pain and suffering of the coming of the Kingdom of God?

And what of the Church, the Body of Christ? I once saw in a

village church some splendid banners portraying lively scenes of local life. The 'church' banner, however, displayed an excellent picture of the church building, with the choir lined up outside – identical faces, identical clothing, feet firmly together and hands demurely still. Is this our picture of the Church – stiff, static, formal and conforming?

Contrast this with the Olympic gymnasts: their incredible swings and somersaults on the rings, flying through the air, turning, twisting, and confidently grasping the rings again for the next movement. Or the so-called floor exercises, when the gymnasts spend their time spinning, twisting and somersaulting in mid-air, or dancing over the floor without seeming to touch it, in movements too quick for the eye to follow, full of dynamism and energy, taking risks, using every muscle in their bodies. When I have shared this image with others they have added words like 'grace', 'suppleness' and 'discipline' to describe the gymnasts' activities. The cynic was quick to point out that some gymnasts injure, even distort, their bodies. Fair comment! The Church too is vulnerable, even to the point of self-inflicted injuries. Why is the Church, the Body of the life-giving Christ, not more like the Olympic gymnasts, full of dynamism and energy, taking risks, and really using all its limbs and organs? Surely Christians believe in the renewing life of the resurrection and the transforming work of the Holy Spirit?

Soon after the 1988 Olympics a Henry Moore exhibition was held at the Royal Academy. Here were sculptures of the human body, remarkable for their greater-than-human size, their curious perspectives, unexpected angles, lack of symmetry, sometimes their very disjointedness, with head or limbs seemingly disconnected from the torso, yet all of a piece. What was Henry Moore trying to express? These bodies claimed attention, provoked questions, compelled reflection. What might they add to our understanding of the image of the Body of Christ?

As the Olympic gymnasts and the Henry Moore sculptures contribute to a new understanding of the Church as the Body of Christ, I see new opportunities opening up for Reader ministry. Such an understanding demands a response from Readers which is open and adventurous, and which leads to new risks and a new vulnerability. Readers must always be listening and learning, and interpreting the gospel so that God may be known among all peoples. For the human face of God takes into account both the diversity and the uniqueness of human beings. It compels Readers to see people of differing creeds, colours and classes *as* they are and *where* they are. It invites Readers to listen to the voice of God in them, in their joys and their sorrows, and to share their own understanding. It also involves standing alongside those who are searching for faith, and those who seem unaware of God's love and compassion. As Readers celebrate their 125th anniversary, they are already poised to step forward, with all God's people, into that future towards which God is already beckoning.